MW00395412

THE SISTER'S SECRETS
a COLLECTION of TIMELESS RECIPES

Susan Lipper

Nancy Pierron

ISBN Number: 0-9722310-0-5

First Printing   October, 2002   5,000 copies

Published by Susan Lipper and Nancy Pierron

All rights reserved. No part of this book may be reproduced or utilized in any form or by any means, electronic, or mechanical, including photocopying, recording, or by any information storage or retrieval system, without the permission in writing from the Publisher.

Please use the order forms located in the back of the book for reorders.

All photography by
William Heroy of EYE-IMPACT
Kathryn Kelly, Creative Director/Designer
320 South Elm Street
Greensboro, North Carolina
Phone (336) 273-1097

WIMMER
COOKBOOKS
ConsolidatedGraphics
1-800-548-2537

DEDICATION

To all the incredible people, good friends, and church family at Mount Pisgah United Methodist Church for their overwhelming generosity and encouragement.

TABLE OF CONTENTS

ACKNOWLEGEMENTS

This all began as we were leaving our business Le Petit Café in Columbia, Missouri. Over the years friends had asked us for recipes and told us we needed to write a cookbook. We thought it was a great idea! Years passed and somehow the project was pushed aside.

I moved to Greensboro, North Carolina and became involved with Mount Pisgah United Methodist Church, the Agape Sunday school class, and cooking for the Wednesday Night Live dinner program.

Our Sunday school class had a picnic, one Sunday afternoon, at the home of Stan and Maggie Tennant. I prepared the Banana Crunch Cake and Chicken Wild Rice Salad as my contribution. Our conversation turned to recipes and who-brought-what, and how-do-you make-this, etc. We have Molly King to thank for suggesting we write a cookbook and reminding us that we needed to continue with our project. I called Susan that same Sunday night in August and said, "we've got to do this and this time we are going to do it. You have to move to Greensboro." This book is the result.

Thank you to our loyal customers of Le Petit Café, in Columbia Missouri, for their support and ideas in writing the cookbook.

We are eternally grateful to the Agape Sunday school class for their prayers, presence, and gifts.

Thank you to Bob Nix, our gift from heaven, for his computer expertise when we (being computer illiterate) were so desperate.

Thank you to Paul, Michael, and Elizabeth Pierron. Even when they were impatient with us for being computer illiterate they freely gave advice.

To Our sister Patricia (Lipper) Self for attending the Wimmer cookbook conference with Susan. Her enthusiasm, encouragement and assistance with the typing sped our completion of this book.

We are grateful to our friend, of 25 years, Polly Musacchia. As an English teacher we relied on her for editing and proofing sections of our cookbook.

To our brother Michael Lipper and sister-in-law Meg, thank you for all the years of critical taste testing while experimenting with different foods.

A poignant heartfelt thank you to Mr. Calvin Kessler of Kessler Industries and his entire staff of remarkable people, including the sales representatives who are located nationwide. These are the people who make the High Point Furniture Market so much fun, despite all the hard work and long hours everyone contributes!

And a special thank you to our parents for enrolling us in the 4-H program where ultimately our cooking and baking skills began.

FOREWORD

Let me tell you a little bit about my sisters and their secrets.

I am the only brother of four older sisters. We were raised on a farm in Missouri during the 1960s. The kitchen in our farmhouse was a massive room with a multi-purpose table. It was used to eat on, bake and mix on, cut long strands of home-made noodles on, and knead bread on. This was all in a time when can openers were only used to open canned foods, not cans of food.

My Mom remembers the first time she realized that her daughters might be interested in cooking. She came in to the kitchen and found them stirring a bag of heart candies in a huge bowl of flour in the middle of the kitchen floor. Years later, when Susan was nine years old, she entered a loaf of bread in the IGA-Clark County Bread Baking Contest. This was a countywide contest and was entered by farm wives who had been baking bread longer than my sister had lived. Needless to say, she won 1st place. I can still see her standing by the propane tank in the back yard as my Dad used the new Polaroid camera to take her picture with the loaf of bread and her big blue ribbon. To my Dad, that day his daughter might as well have won a gold medal in the Olympics.

There were probably several hundred cookies baked every season for school parties, church socials, and plates to the neighbors. If I was quick enough, I could snag a few scraps without getting my hand slapped away. My Dad's excuse was that he had to check every batch to make sure they were good enough. I have learned well from my father; I use that ploy yet today.

By now my Mom was used to issuing orders and shopping for groceries and my sisters ran the kitchen. Susan was the last of the sisters to leave from home. When she left, it was a sad day for my Dad and me. Mom hardly remembered where the pans were, let alone what that thing with the four burners did.

The bottom line is, my sisters are exceptional cooks. Their secret is they love it. Flour runs through their veins in a thin, but creamy roux with no lumps. They have a knack for it and a story to tell from every catering and every dish that they have ever created. If you want to try something new for supper and want it to be really delicious, it's in here. If you want to take something easy and delicious across the street to a friend's house for supper, it's in here. If it is your turn to host Thanksgiving dinner for all the in-laws, this book has recipes to impress even the crustiest of mothers-in-law. Go ahead, take this one home with you and try out any page. Spend some time in the kitchen again. It will be well worth your time and effort when you sit down and really enjoy the flavor of a delicious meal.

Bon Appetit,
Michael Lipper
Official taster of all the Lipper Sister's creations

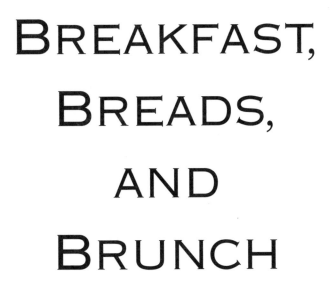

Breakfast, Breads, and Brunch

Surprise Buns

Surprise! The center is hollow and delicious. As children, when we stayed with our grandparents during the summer, these were a special treat for us.

2 dozen

1	package yeast
¼	cup lukewarm water
1	teaspoon granulated sugar
¾	cup milk
¼	cup granulated sugar
1	teaspoon salt
1	egg
¼	cup vegetable shortening or unsalted butter
3½-4 cups all-purpose flour	
½	cup unsalted butter or margarine, melted
½	cup granulated sugar
1	teaspoon cinnamon
24	large marshmallows

Combine yeast, water and 1 teaspoon sugar. Let set 5 minutes for yeast to activate. Heat milk to lukewarm and combine with the yeast mixture. Add ¼ cup sugar, salt, egg, and shortening. Mix well. Stir in enough flour for a soft pliable dough.

Knead on a smooth surface, adding more flour if needed until dough is soft, but not sticky. Knead for 5 minutes, or until dough is springy and smooth. Place in a buttered bowl and turn dough to butter all sides to keep moist. Cover and let rise until double. Punch down and let rise 30 minutes more.

Turn out onto a counter and roll to ¼ inch thick. Cut into 3-inch circles. Combine melted butter, ½ cup sugar, and cinnamon. Dip each marshmallow into this and place in center of the dough. Bring dough around marshmallows, pinching to seal the seam. Dip top into cinnamon mixture. Place pinched side down, into a generously buttered muffin pan. Let rise until almost double, about 30 to 40 minutes.

Preheat oven to 375°. Bake 20 to 25 minutes.

Spiced Pumpkin Loaf

Makes 1 loaf

1¾	cups all-purpose flour
1	teaspoon baking powder
1	teaspoon baking soda
½	teaspoon salt
1	cup canned pumpkin purée
⅔	cup granulated sugar
⅓	cup sour cream
⅓	cup vegetable oil
1	egg
3	tablespoons orange marmalade
1	teaspoon ground cinnamon
½	teaspoon ground ginger
¼	teaspoon ground nutmeg
⅛	teaspoon ground cloves
⅔	cup chopped walnuts

Preheat oven to 350°.

Butter a 9x5-inch loaf pan and line with parchment paper.

Sift flour, baking powder, baking soda and salt in medium bowl and set aside. Combine pumpkin, sugar, sour cream, oil, egg, marmalade, cinnamon, ginger, nutmeg and cloves in large bowl of electric mixer and stir on medium speed to blend. Reduce speed to low and gradually blend in flour mixture. Stir in nuts. Transfer batter to prepared pan, smoothing top. Bake until tester inserted in center comes out clean, about 65 minutes.

Let cool in pan on rack 10 minutes. Remove loaf from pan and discard parchment paper. Let cool completely on rack.

All the following bread recipes in this chapter are excellent served with a flavored cream cheese. We recommend orange, strawberry, or raspberry flavors.

Lemon Bread

Makes 2 loaves.

Bread

2	cups granulated sugar
1	cup unsalted butter, at room temperature
4	eggs
	Fine grated zest of 2 lemons
3	cups all-purpose flour
2½	teaspoons baking powder
1	teaspoon salt
½	cup milk
½	cup fresh lemon juice

Glaze

½	cup fresh lemon juice
½	cup granulated sugar

Bread

Preheat oven to 350°. Butter a 9x5-inch loaf pan and line with parchment paper.

Cream sugar and butter until light and fluffy. Add eggs, lemon zest, and continue to beat. Sift the dry ingredients and add alternately with the milk and lemon juice. Blend until batter is smooth. Pour into prepared pans and bake 40 to 45 minutes, or until a tester inserted in the center comes out clean.

Glaze

While the bread is baking, prepare the glaze. In a non-reactive saucepan, heat the lemon juice and sugar until the sugar is dissolved. Remove the bread from the oven, and brush the warm glaze over the top. Let the bread absorb the glaze and cool before removing from the pans.

Apple Bread

1 loaf

2	eggs
1	cup granulated sugar
½	cup vegetable oil
1	teaspoon vanilla
2	cups peeled, cored, and grated apples
2	cups all-purpose flour
½	teaspoon soda
1	teaspoon baking powder
½	teaspoon salt
1½	teaspoons cinnamon
½	teaspoon nutmeg

Preheat oven to 350°. Butter a 9x5-inch loaf pan and line with parchment paper.

Beat together the eggs, sugar, oil and vanilla. Add apples, then stir in the dry ingredients. Mix together until well blended. Pour into prepared pan and bake until dark brown and slightly domed in the center and firm to touch.

This freezes well, and mellows in flavor. It is always better served a day or two after it is baked.

Cranberry Apple Tea Bread

2 loaves

½	cup unsalted butter, at room temperature
1¾	cups granulated sugar
4	large eggs
1	pint (2 cups) sour cream
4	teaspoons fine grated lemon zest
6	cups all-purpose flour (weight 28 ounces)
7½	teaspoons baking powder
1	teaspoon baking soda
1	teaspoon salt
1	(12-ounce) bag fresh cranberries, coarsely chopped
3	apples, peeled, cored and chopped
1	cup toasted, pecan pieces

Preheat oven to 350°. Butter and line 2 (9x5-inch) loaf pans with parchment paper.

Cream butter and sugar until fluffy. Add eggs, and continue beating 2 minutes. Stir in sour cream and zest. Sift together flour, baking powder, baking soda, and salt. Add to butter mixture.

Fold in cranberries, apples, and nuts. Spoon into prepared pans and bake 60 to 70 minutes until a cake tester inserted in the center comes out clean. Cool 10 minutes before removing from pans.

Refrigerate bread 24 hours before serving.

It is important to measure the flour accurately. Using less than 6 cups or 28 ounces will result in a dense texture and the bread will not peak.

The Best Banana Bread

1 large loaf

½	cup unsalted butter, at room temperature
1½	cups granulated sugar
1	teaspoon vanilla
2	egg yolks
1	cup mashed over-ripe bananas
¾	teaspoon baking soda
½	cup buttermilk
2	cups all-purpose flour
½	teaspoon salt
½	teaspoon baking powder
2	egg whites

Preheat oven to 350°. Line a 9x5-inch loaf pan with parchment paper.

Beat the butter, sugar, vanilla and egg yolks together until light and fluffy. Add the bananas.

Mix together the baking soda and buttermilk, then add to the banana mixture, alternating with the dry ingredients; flour, salt, and baking powder.

Whip remaining egg whites to soft peaks. Fold into banana batter until whites are completely incorporated. Pour into prepared pan. Bake 55 to 60 minutes until a tester inserted in the center comes out clean. The crust should be golden brown on top and slightly spongy to touch.

The center does not dome. This is best after it has set for a day or has been frozen.

Delicious served with whipped strawberry butter or cream cheese.

Poppyseed Bread

2 loaves

2¼	cups milk
1¾	cups vegetable oil
4	eggs
3½	cups granulated sugar
2	teaspoons vanilla
2	teaspoons almond extract
4½	cups all-purpose flour
2¼	teaspoons salt
2¼	teaspoons baking powder
2	tablespoons poppyseeds

Preheat oven to 350°. Line 2 (9x5-inch) loaf pans with parchment paper.

In a large mixing bowl with a wire whip, stir together the milk, oil, eggs, sugar, vanilla and almond extract until smooth. Add the flour, salt, baking powder and poppyseeds and continue mixing at a low speed until all flour is well blended and mixture is smooth.

Pour into prepared pans. Bake 30 to 40 minutes until center peaks and tester inserted in the center comes out clean.

Center should dome and top of loaves should be golden brown.

Zucchini Date Nut Bread
1 loaf

2	eggs
1	cup granulated sugar
½	cup vegetable oil
1	cup unpeeled grated zucchini
1	cup walnut pieces
¾	cup chopped dates
1¾	cups all-purpose flour
1	teaspoon baking powder
1	teaspoon ground cinnamon
½	teaspoon baking soda
½	teaspoon ground cardamom
½	teaspoon ground allspice
¼	teaspoon salt

Preheat oven to 350°. Butter a 9x5-inch loaf pan or line with parchment paper.

In a large mixing bowl, mix the eggs, sugar, oil, and zucchini together. Add the nuts and dates. Sift together the dry ingredients and add to the liquids; stir until well blended.

Bake 50 to 60 minutes or until tester inserted in the center comes out clean.

Orange Zucchini Bread

2 loaves

4	eggs
1	cup vegetable oil
2	cups granulated sugar
4	cups unpeeled zucchini, grated
3	cups all-purpose flour
4	teaspoons baking powder
1	teaspoons baking soda
½	teaspoon salt
½	teaspoon ground ginger
2	teaspoons finely grated orange zest
1	cup toasted pecan pieces

Preheat oven to 350°. Line 2 (9x5-inch) loaf pans with parchment paper.

Mix eggs, oil, sugar, and zucchini. Sift together the flour, baking powder, soda, salt and ginger. Add to egg mixture, then mix in orange zest and nuts. Mix until blended, and pour into prepared loaf pans.

Bake 50 to 60 minutes or until a tester inserted in the center comes out clean.

Sausage Bread

This is a delicious bread to serve as a tea sandwich spread with cream cheese.
We suggest using Jimmy Dean sausage for best flavor.

2 loaves

1	cup dark raisins
1	pound raw hot spicy sausage
1	cup toasted pecan pieces
1½	cups packed light brown sugar
1½	cups granulated sugar
2	eggs
3	cups all-purpose flour
1	teaspoon ground ginger
1	teaspoon pumpkin pie spice
1	teaspoon baking powder
1	teaspoon baking soda
1	cup cold coffee

Preheat oven to 350°. Line 2 (9x5-inch) loaf pans with parchment paper.

Cover raisins in hot water to plump. Drain and discard liquid.

Mix sausage, sugar and eggs. Stir in nuts and raisins. Measure flour, spices, and baking powder together. Stir soda into coffee and blend into sausage mixture. Add dry ingredients and blend well. Pour into prepared pans and bake 1 hour until a tester inserted in the center comes out clean.

Mexican Corn Bread

3	eggs
½	cup vegetable oil
1	cup white onion, diced
1	finely chopped green bell pepper
3	tablespoons granulated sugar
1	can Mexicorn, drained
1	cup grated sharp Cheddar cheese
	Jalapeño peppers (3 for mild, 4 for medium, 6 for hot)
3	cups White Lily Self-Rising Cornmeal mix
2	cups buttermilk

Preheat oven to 350°. Butter a 9x13-inch pan.

Combine the eggs and oil in a bowl. Add the onions, green pepper, sugar, Mexicorn and cheese. Finely mince the jalapeño peppers and add to the mixture. Stir in the cornmeal mix and buttermilk blending well. Pour into prepared pan. Bake 25 to 30 minutes until a tester inserted in the center comes out clean and bread is firm in the center.

Mast Farm Inn Cornbread

Dr. Randy Lewis and his wife Pam are members of our Agape Sunday school class. As sponsors of the Sudanese Lost Boys we have heard stories of excitement and frustration about the Boys and how they are learning to speak English and adjust to the American culture. During the Lewis' hectic schedule they have taken the time to share with us their favorite recipe, which happens to be from the Mast Farm Inn Cookbook.

1	scant cup self-rising cornmeal
1	scant cup unbleached all-purpose flour
1	teaspoon baking powder
½	teaspoon baking soda
½	teaspoon salt
1	tablespoon granulated sugar (optional)
2	eggs
2	cups buttermilk
¼	cup corn oil

Preheat oven to 425°. Grease a 10-inch pyrex pie plate or iron skillet.

Measure cornmeal, flour, baking soda, salt, and sugar into a sifter.

Whisk eggs, buttermilk, and oil together in a large mixing bowl.

Sift dry ingredients into liquids and beat until smooth and well blended.

Pour mixture into skillet or pie plate and bake for 20 minutes or until nicely browned.

Dr. Randy Lewis

Frozen Biscuits

We asked our Aunt Rovene Lipper for a few of her easy,
but wonderful recipes she would like to contribute to our cookbook.
She has collected thousands of recipes over the past few decades, and stores
them in file cabinets. These biscuits are worthy to grace any breakfast table.
The cream of tartar and egg produce tender fluffy biscuits.

2 dozen

2	cups sifted unbleached all-purpose flour
4	teaspoons baking powder
½	teaspoon cream of tartar
½	teaspoon salt
2	tablespoons granulated sugar
½	cup shortening
⅔	cup milk
1	beaten egg

Combine dry ingredients, then cut in shortening. Add milk and beaten egg and
mix well. Turn out onto a floured surface and knead 5 times. Roll out to ½-inch
thickness. Using a cutter cut straight down, not a back and forth motion. This
prevents biscuits from rising uniformly. Place on a baking sheet and freeze. When
frozen, place in plastic bag to use as needed.

When ready to bake place biscuits on a paper lined baking sheet and thaw. Bake at
450° 10 to 15 minutes until golden brown.

Herbed Buttermilk Biscuits

20 biscuits

3	cups unbleached all-purpose flour
2	tablespoons granulated sugar
1	teaspoon salt
2	tablespoons baking powder
¾	teaspoon baking soda
½	cup vegetable shortening
½	cup cold unsalted butter
4	tablespoons unsalted butter
1	small onion, minced
2	garlic cloves, minced
2	tablespoons minced parsley
2	tablespoons minced fresh dill
⅓	cup celery leaves, minced
⅔	cup buttermilk
¼	cup whipping cream

The day before serving, cut shortening and butter into dry ingredients. Mixture should be crumbly. Cover and refrigerate overnight.

Preheat oven to 400°.

Sauté butter and onion in a skillet for about 5 to 6 minutes. Add remaining ingredients and continue to sauté another 4 to 5 minutes. Remove from heat and cool to room temperature.

Stir onion herb mixture into buttermilk and cream. Mix in chilled dry crumb mixture just enough to form a dough. Turn out onto a floured surface and knead 3 times.

Roll out to ¾-inch thickness. Cut out and place on a paper-lined baking sheet

Bake 12 to 15 minutes until light golden brown. Serve with butter.

Sweet Potato Rolls

Our sister Patricia remembers the time in 4-H when she and Nancy entered a
loaf of bread in the fair. Patricia had baked a loaf of white bread to enter.
Nancy realized she did not have time to bake a loaf before the judging deadline
so Patricia cut the bread in half and they each entered halves of the same bread.
The judges awarded Nancy the blue ribbon and Patricia the red ribbon!
She still has not recovered from that fiasco.

2 to 3 dozen

1	cup warm water
1	cup warm milk
3	packages dry yeast
¾	cup vegetable shortening or margarine
2	cups cooked mashed sweet potatoes
¾	cup packed light brown sugar
1	tablespoon baking powder
1	tablespoon salt
5	eggs
9-11	cups bread flour

Dissolve yeast in water and milk. Set aside 5 minutes to activate. Add remaining
ingredients, mixing in enough flour to form a soft dough. Knead until smooth and
elastic, about 10 minutes. Let dough rise in a warm draft-free area until doubled in
size, about 1 hour. Punch down and shape into round rolls.

Place on a lightly buttered or paper lined baking sheet; let rise 30 to 40 minutes.

Preheat oven to 350°. Rolls should feel soft and spongy when ready to bake. Bake
15 to 20 minutes until golden.

Sweet Potato Biscuits

These are dense and aromatic, perfect for serving with ham or turkey.
They made their debut at the wedding reception of Stacy Cohan and Jay Yates.
The small cocktail size biscuits were sandwiched with honey mustard and
smoked ham. They were well received and quickly consumed.

As a biscuit they can be shaped in a cocktail size or larger
and spread with honey spice butter.

12 biscuits

¾   cup cooked, peeled and mashed sweet potato
2   tablespoons whipping cream
½   teaspoon fine grated lemon zest
½   cup cold unsalted butter
1½   cups unbleached all-purpose flour
½   teaspoon salt
2½   teaspoons baking powder
½   teaspoon ground cinnamon
¼   teaspoon allspice
¼   teaspoon ground nutmeg
¼   cup packed light brown sugar

Glaze
1   egg
1   tablespoon whipping cream

Biscuits

Preheat oven to 450°.

Mix together sweet potato, cream, and lemon zest; set aside.

Sift together dry ingredients. Cut butter into dry ingredients until mixture resembles coarse meal. Add potato mixture to crumb mixture and stir just until evenly moistened. Turn out onto a floured surface and knead gently to form dough.

Divide dough in half and pat each piece to ¾-inch thickness. Cut each piece into six servings, cutting straight down, not a back-and-forth motion; it prevents biscuits from rising uniformly.

Sweet Potato Biscuits continued

Glaze

Whisk the egg with the cream and brush tops with glaze. Bake about 12 to 13 minutes until golden brown. Serve warm.

It is necessary to use cold butter to prevent the dry ingredients from forming a soft mass of dough. The biscuits do not rise properly and the texture is heavy.

Banana Cream Breakfast Cake

1 cake

Filling

2	(3-ounce) packages cream cheese
⅓	cup granulated sugar
1	tablespoon all-purpose flour
½	teaspoon ground nutmeg
1	egg

Cake

½	cup unsalted butter, at room temperature
1½	cups granulated sugar
2	eggs
1	teaspoon vanilla
1	teaspoon baking soda
3	tablespoons hot water
3	cups cake flour
1	teaspoon baking powder
½	teaspoon salt
½	teaspoon ground nutmeg
½	teaspoon ground cinnamon
⅓	cup orange juice
3	over-ripe bananas, mashed
1	cup toasted pecan pieces

Glaze

1	tablespoon unsalted butter, melted
1	tablespoon granulated sugar
¼	teaspoon ground cinnamon

Filling

Preheat oven to 350°. Butter and flour a Bundt pan or a 10-inch tube pan.

Beat cream cheese, sugar, flour, and nutmeg together until smooth. Blend in the egg. Set cheese mixture aside.

Banana Cream Breakfast Cake continued

Cake

Cream together the butter and sugar until pale and fluffy. Add eggs and vanilla and continue beating. Stir together the soda and hot water, then add to the butter mixture. Sift together the flour, baking powder, salt, nutmeg, and cinnamon. Alternately add the dry ingredients to the butter mixture with the orange juice. Stir in bananas and pecans.

Spoon half the batter into the prepared pan. Spread the cream cheese mixture over the batter. Carefully spread remaining batter over cream cheese. Bake 50 to 55 minutes until tester inserted in the center comes out clean.

Glaze

Mix together ingredients for glaze and set aside. Cool cake and release from pan. Brush cake with glaze.

Pumpkin Coffee Cake

1 Bundt cake

Pecan Topping

⅓	cup packed brown sugar
¼	cup granulated sugar
1	teaspoon ground cinnamon
1	cup toasted pecan pieces

Cake

1	cup unsalted butter, at room temperature
1½	cups granulated sugar
1	teaspoon vanilla
2	eggs
1	cup canned pumpkin purée
¼	cup sour cream
3	cups cake flour
1	teaspoon baking powder
½	teaspoon baking soda
½	teaspoon salt
1	teaspoon ground ginger
½	teaspoon ground nutmeg
1	teaspoon ground cinnamon

Topping

Preheat oven to 350°. Butter and flour a Bundt pan or a 10-inch tube pan.

Mix together the topping ingredients, then set aside.

Cake

Cream together the butter, sugar, and vanilla until smooth, add the eggs, pumpkin, and sour cream. Sift together the flour, baking powder, soda, salt, ginger, nutmeg, and cinnamon. Stir into the creamed mixture mixing until batter is smooth.

Spread half of batter into the prepared pan. Sprinkle with half of the pecan topping. Spread remaining batter on top, then sprinkle with remaining pecan topping. Bake 50 to 55 minutes until a tester inserted in the center comes out clean. Cool and remove from pan.

Blueberry Sour Cream Cake

1 Bundt cake

Streusel Topping

1	cup packed light brown sugar
1	teaspoon ground cinnamon
1	cup toasted pecan or walnut pieces

Cake

½	cup unsalted butter, at room temperature
1	cup granulated sugar
1	teaspoon vanilla
3	eggs
1	(8-ounce) carton dairy sour cream
2	cups cake flour
1	teaspoon baking soda
1	teaspoon salt
1	cups fresh or frozen blueberries

Streusel Topping

Preheat oven to 350°. Butter and flour a Bundt pan or 10-inch tube pan.

Mix together topping ingredients and set aside.

Cake

On an electric mixer beat together the butter, sugar, vanilla, then add eggs. Beat until smooth and fluffy. Stir in sour cream. Sift together flour, soda, and salt. Stir until well blended. Remove from mixer and fold in blueberries.

Spread ½ of the batter into the prepared pan, and layer with ½ of the Streusel Topping. Spread remaining batter on top, and then sprinkle with remaining topping mixture. Bake 35 to 40 minutes or until cake tester inserted in the center comes out clean.

Zucchini Carrot Coffee Cake

12 to 16 servings

Cake

½	cup unsalted butter, at room temperature
1¼	cups packed light brown sugar
½	cup vegetable oil
2	eggs
2	cups grated raw carrots
1	cup grated raw unpeeled zucchini
1	cup all-purpose flour
1	cup whole wheat flour
1	tablespoon baking powder
1½	teaspoons baking soda
½	teaspoon ground cinnamon
1	teaspoon ground nutmeg
1	teaspoon salt

Streusel Topping

6	tablespoons packed brown sugar
6	tablespoons granulated sugar
½	cup all-purpose flour
¼	teaspoon salt
½	teaspoon ground cinnamon
6	tablespoons cold unsalted butter
½	cup pecan pieces

Cake

Preheat oven to 350°. Butter a 9x13-inch pan.

On an electric mixer beat butter and brown sugar together until fluffy. Stir in oil and eggs, then carrots and zucchini. Add remaining ingredients and blend well. Pour into prepared 9x13-inch pan and sprinkle with Streusel Topping. Bake 20 to 25 minutes or until tester inserted in center comes out clean.

Streusel Topping

Using a pastry cutter, mix all ingredients until crumbly. Do not over mix; streusel should still be dry and crumbly, not a soft dough.

Banana Nut Muffins

I have been making these muffins for 10 years. During a visit to my good friends, the Musacchia's, Polly and I were having coffee one morning and searching through her recipe file she found the muffin recipe and remembered how flavorful they are. She shared her banana muffin recipe with me. Once I happened to have fresh blueberries that needed to be used, and we now prefer the muffins with blueberries for a different flavor combination.

12 muffins

1	egg
3	tablespoons milk
½	cup unsalted butter, melted
1¼	cups mashed overripe bananas
¾	cup toasted pecan pieces
1½	cups unbleached all-purpose flour
1½	teaspoons baking soda
¼	teaspoon salt
¾	cup granulated sugar
1	cup fresh or frozen blueberries or strawberries (optional)

Preheat oven to 375°.

Mix together the egg, milk, and butter. Add bananas and pecans. Sift together flour soda salt, and sugar. Fold dry ingredients into banana mixture just to moisten flour. At this point carefully fold in desired fruit.

Do not over mix.

Divide batter into 12 paper-lined muffin cups. Bake 18 to 20 minutes. Cool, then sprinkle with powdered sugar if desired

These mellow in flavor when served the next day; they also freeze well.

It is very important not to over mix the batter. Muffins are tough when batter is well blended.

Nancy (Lipper) Pierron

Blueberry Streusel Muffins

12 muffins

½   cup granulated sugar
¼   cup unsalted butter, at room temperature
1   egg
1   teaspoon vanilla
2⅓   cups unbleached all-purpose flour
4   teaspoons baking powder
½   teaspoon salt
1   cup milk
1¾   cups fresh or frozen blueberries

Topping
½   cup granulated sugar
⅓   cup all-purpose flour
1   teaspoon ground cinnamon
¼   cup unsalted butter, melted

Muffins
Preheat oven to 375°.

Cream together the sugar and butter; then add the egg and vanilla. Stir in dry ingredients alternately with the milk. Gently and carefully fold in blueberries to combine.

Divide batter into 12 paper-lined muffin cups. Sprinkle streusel on top of muffins. Bake 20 to 25 minutes. Muffins will crack on top and be firm in the center when done.

Streusel Topping
Combine all the topping ingredients to a crumb mixture.

To avoid discolored batter, do not over-mix the blueberries.

Lemon Yogurt Muffins

12 muffins

Muffins

2	cups unbleached all-purpose flour
1	teaspoon baking powder
1	teaspoon baking soda
½	teaspoon salt
2	eggs
1¼	cups plain yogurt
¼	cup unsalted butter, melted, cooled
¼	cup granulated sugar
2	tablespoons honey
1	tablespoon fine grated lemon zest

Lemon Syrup

⅓	cup fresh lemon juice
⅓	cup granulated sugar
3	tablespoons water

Muffins

Preheat oven to 375°.

With a wire whisk, stir flour, baking powder, soda, and salt. In a separate bowl, whisk eggs, yogurt, butter, ¼ cup sugar, honey and lemon zest. Fold in dry ingredients just to moisten. Spoon into buttered or paper-lined muffin cups. Bake 15 to 20 minutes until muffins peak and feel firm in the center.

Syrup

While muffins are baking, stir together the syrup ingredients. When muffins are done, pierce the tops of muffins several times with a fork or skewer. Brush syrup over tops of muffins. Let cool in pan 3 minutes before serving.

Maple Pecan Scones

12 scones

3½	cups unbleached all-purpose flour
1	cup finely chopped pecans
4	teaspoons baking powder
1	teaspoon salt
¾	cup cold unsalted butter
1	cup milk
½	cup real maple syrup, divided

Preheat oven to 425°.

With pastry cutter cut butter into dry ingredients and pecans until mixture resembles coarse crumbs. Add milk and 5 tablespoons maple syrup. Mix lightly until mixture clings together and forms a ball.

Turn dough out onto lightly floured surface; knead 5 to 6 times. Roll out one inch thick and cut out scones in circles or desired shape. Place on a buttered or parchment paper-lined baking sheet.

Brush tops of scones with remaining maple syrup and sprinkle with extra chopped pecans. Bake 15 to 18 minutes or until light golden brown and firm. Brush scones with any remaining syrup. Serve warm with butter.

Whole Wheat Scones

12 scones

2	cups unsifted stone-ground whole-wheat flour
2	cups unsifted unbleached all-purpose flour
3	tablespoons packed light brown sugar
4	teaspoons baking powder
1	teaspoon salt
1	cup cold unsalted butter
½	cup golden raisins (optional)
1⅓	cups milk
2	tablespoons unprocessed bran
2	tablespoons milk for glaze

Preheat oven to 425°.

In a large bowl, combine flours, sugar, baking powder, and salt. With a pastry blender, cut in butter until mixture resembles coarse crumbs. Stir in raisins, if desired. Add 1⅓ cups milk to crumb mixture. Stir until mixture forms soft dough.

On a floured surface, gently knead dough 4 to 5 times. Divide dough in half. Roll dough into a circle 1-inch thick. Brush tops with the 2 tablespoons milk and sprinkle with bran. Cut into 6 wedges. Repeat with remaining dough. Place scones 1-inch apart on a buttered or parchment paper-lined baking sheet. Bake 15 to 18 minutes or until golden brown and firm in the center. Serve warm.

Unprocessed bran is found in the cereal aisle in grocery stores.

Egg Brunch Casserole

We dislike the word casserole, but it best describes this dish. It is excellent served with garlic cheese grits and a scone of any flavor, or with the Sweet Potato Biscuits. It can be made the day before, refrigerated and heated when needed. Garnish with grated cheese and chopped green onions if so desired. Mrs. Lyria Bartlett, of Columbia Missouri, graciously shared her recipe with us to use for a catered event. It has been a personal favorite for years.

12 servings

8	slices bacon
1	(8-ounce) container fresh mushrooms, sliced
2	jars sliced dried beef, cut into strips
¼	cup unsalted butter
⅓	cup all-purpose flour
4	cups milk
18	large eggs
	Salt and pepper to taste
1	cup half-and-half

Preheat oven to 275°. Butter a 3-quart casserole dish.

In a large skillet, slowly cook bacon until done. Remove from skillet, cool, and break into pieces. Sauté sliced mushrooms in the same skillet with bacon grease. Add dried beef and chopped bacon; set aside.

In a saucepan, make a white sauce. Melt ¼ cup butter, and stir in the flour. While whisking constantly with a wire whisk, add 4 cups milk. Cook until thickened and add meat and mushroom mixture. Remove from heat.

In a separate bowl, mix eggs, salt, pepper, and half-and-half. Scramble in a skillet.

Put half of scrambled egg mixture in prepared dish, and then pour half of sauce over eggs. Repeat with eggs, then top with remaining sauce. Bake covered with a lid or foil for 30 minutes to heat through.

Spinach and Gruyère Puff

Another perfect brunch idea; serve with a scone,
muffin or fruit for a refreshing start to your day.

12 servings

1	small leek, including green tops
1	tablespoon olive oil
2	teaspoons minced garlic
8	ounces fresh baby spinach, washed and dried
1½	teaspoons salt
1	teaspoon ground black pepper
¼	teaspoon ground nutmeg
2¼	cups milk
¾	cup finely ground cornmeal
4	ounces Gruyère cheese, rind removed, grated or Swiss cheese
½	cup grated Parmesan cheese
4	egg yolks
6	egg whites

Preheat oven to 375°. Butter a 9x13-inch pan.

Thinly slice leeks and place in a bowl of water to rinse. Let the sediment settle to the bottom and lift out of water. Rinse again if needed. Set aside. In a large sauté pan or skillet over medium heat, cook leeks in oil and garlic until soft. Add spinach and sauté until wilted; 2 to 4 minutes. Season with salt, pepper, and nutmeg. Remove from heat and set aside.

In a 2-quart saucepan over medium heat, scald milk. Whisk in cornmeal and cook, stirring constantly, 10 minutes. Stir in cheeses and season with salt and pepper. Cover and cool 5 minutes.

Fold yolks into cornmeal mixture, then fold in spinach. On an electric mixer with the whip attachment, whip whites to soft peaks. Fold ⅓ of the whites into cornmeal mixture to lighten batter. Fold in remaining whites. Pour into prepared pan and bake 25 minutes until puffed and golden brown. Serve immediately.

Any refrigerated leftover puff retains its moist texture reheated in the microwave.

Garlic Cheese Grits

8 to 10 servings

2	cups grits
2	cups grated Cheddar cheese
2	tablespoons minced fresh garlic
½	cup unsalted butter
1	bunch green onions, chopped fine
	Salt and pepper to taste
⅛	teaspoon hot sauce

Preheat oven to 400°.

Cook grits according to directions on package. Add the grated cheese, garlic, butter, onion, and seasonings to taste. Place in a buttered 1-quart casserole and bake 45 minutes. Garnish with extra grated cheese and green onions.

Soups
and Salads
with
their
Dressings

SOUPS AND SALADS WITH THEIR DRESSINGS

Tulsa Tomato Soup

6 servings

3	large leeks, thinly sliced
½	cup (1 stick) unsalted butter
6	large tomatoes (2½ to 3 pounds), peeled, seeded and chopped
2	teaspoons salt
½	teaspoon instant coffee powder
6	cups chicken broth
2-3	tablespoons tomato paste
3	tablespoons chopped fresh basil or 1 tablespoon dried, crumbled
½	cup heavy whipping cream
2	egg yolks
	Chopped fresh chives (garnish)

Rinse leeks in a bowl of water. Let the sediment settle to the bottom and lift out of water. Repeat if necessary. Melt butter in large saucepan over medium-low heat. Add leeks. Cover and cook until softened, about 10 minutes. Stir in tomatoes, salt and coffee powder. Increase heat to medium and cook 10 minutes, stirring occasionally. Add broth, tomato paste and basil and cook 25 minutes. Transfer mixture to processor or blender in batches and purée. Return to saucepan.

Soup can be prepared 1 day ahead to this point. Let cool, then cover and refrigerate. Reheat before proceeding with recipe.

Just before serving, whisk cream and yolks in medium bowl. Gradually whisk 1 cup hot soup into yolk mixture, then whisk yolk mixture into soup. Cook over medium heat, stirring constantly, until slightly thickened; do not boil or yolk will curdle. Ladle into bowls. Garnish with chives and serve.

White Chili

12 servings

1	pound great Northern white beans
2	whole chicken breasts
1	tablespoon olive oil
2	medium onions, chopped
4	garlic cloves, minced
2	(4-ounce) cans mild green chilies, minced, or use 4 fresh jalapeño or other
	hot peppers
2	teaspoons ground cumin
1½	teaspoons dried oregano
¼	teaspoon cayenne pepper
6	cups chicken stock, or canned chicken broth
12	ounces grated Monterey Jack cheese
	Sour cream
	Other garnishes, such as chopped onions, black olives

Sort and soak the beans overnight in water in a Dutch oven or other pot. The water should be about 3 inches above the beans.

Place the chicken in a heavy Dutch oven. Add cold water to cover. Bring to a boil and simmer 25 minutes. Remove the chicken. Cool chicken slightly and remove the skin from bones and cut the meat into cubes. Reserve the chicken and refrigerate.

Drain beans and remove them to a bowl. Heat oil in the pot you soaked the beans in. Add onions and sauté over medium heat about 8 minutes, stirring frequently. Add garlic, chilies, cumin, oregano, and cayenne. Sauté 2 minutes more. Add beans and stock. Bring to a boil. Reduce heat and simmer for 2 hours, uncovered. Add the chicken and cook 10 minutes. Stir in 1 cup of the cheese and stir until cheese has melted and chicken is heated through. If the chili seems too thin, mix ¼ cup of cornmeal with ½ cup of water. Pour into chili, stirring until thickened. Serve with the remaining cheese, sour cream, and other garnishes on the side.

Make chicken stock by returning the bones and skin to the water the chicken was cooked in. Add an onion, some parsley and celery leaves and simmer, partly covered, for about an hour.

Minestrone

12 servings

6	tablespoons unsalted butter
3	large carrots
2	ribs celery, chopped
2	medium yellow onions, diced
2	garlic cloves, minced
1	medium head green cabbage, chopped
1	(16-ounce) can whole tomatoes
8	cups beef stock
⅓	cup long grain rice (or orzo)
2	teaspoons salt
2	teaspoons Worcestershire sauce
¼	teaspoon oregano
¼	teaspoon black pepper
4	medium potatoes, peeled and cubed
2	beef bouillon cubes
2	large zucchini, cubed
2	(15-ounce) cans kidney beans, drained
1	(10-ounce) package frozen spinach, thawed and drained
	Grated Parmesan or Romano cheese for garnish

In a Dutch oven sauté butter, carrots, celery, onions, garlic, and cabbage 5 minutes. Coarsely chop tomatoes and add with the broth. Bring to a boil and stir in remaining ingredients, except cheese. Simmer 20 minutes or until rice is tender. Ladle into serving bowls and sprinkle with grated cheese.

Lobster and Roasted Sweet Corn Chowder

10 servings

¾	pound (12-ounces) bacon, cut into julienne strips
2	cups chopped yellow onions
1	cup chopped celery
1	cup diced carrots
1½	teaspoons salt
½	teaspoon cayenne pepper
6	bay leaves
¾	cup all-purpose flour
8	cups chicken stock or chicken broth
1½	pounds new potatoes, quartered
1	cup fresh sweet corn, cut from the cob
1	teaspoon crab boil
1	cup half-and-half
½	cup minced fresh parsley
¼	teaspoon hot sauce
1	teaspoon Worcestershire sauce
5	whole main lobsters, cooked and split in half (following recipe)

In large nonstick stockpot, over low heat, cook bacon 10 minutes. Stir in onions, celery, and carrots, and season with salt, cayenne pepper, and bay leaves. Sauté 10 minutes over medium heat, stirring occasionally, until vegetables are very tender. Stir in flour and reduce heat to medium-low. Add 2 tablespoons butter if bacon fat has been absorbed. Cook and stir 2 minutes more. Stir in chicken stock. Bring to boil. Add potatoes and corn. Stir in crab boil. Simmer 15 minutes or until potatoes are fork-tender. Discard bay leaves.

Stir in half-and-half and parsley, hot sauce, and Worcestershire sauce. Simmer 5 minutes. Place half of each lobster in separate bowls. Spoon chowder over lobster meat and serve.

°*Liquid Crab boil, called shrimp boil or fish boil, is found in the seafood department at the supermarket.*

Boiled Lobster

1   tablespoon salt
10   quarts water
5   (1 to 1½-pound) live whole Maine lobsters

In large kettle bring at least 10 quarts salted water to boil. Cook lobsters no more than three at a time. Grasp each lobster just behind eyes; rinse under cold running water. Quickly plunge lobsters headfirst into boiling water. Return water to boil and cook lobsters about 10 to 12 minutes or until they turn orange-red. Drain.

Remove bands or pegs from large claws of cooked lobsters. When cool enough to handle put each lobster on its back. With a heavy knife or kitchen shears, cut body in half lengthwise up to the tail. Cut away membrane on tail to expose meat and small sand sac near head. Remove and discard the sand sac and black vein running through tail. Remove green tomalley (liver) and any coral roe (found in female lobsters). Using a nutcracker, break open the claws. Loosen meat from claws, tail and body. Leave in shells to serve, if desired.

Black Bean Soup with Rum

2	cups chopped onion
1	cup chopped celery
6	sprigs fresh parsley
2	sprigs fresh thyme or ¼ teaspoon crumbled
1	bay leaf
3	tablespoons unsalted butter
1	large ham hock (1¼ pound)
2	cups dry black beans soaked in water overnight and drained
6	cups beef broth
2	cups water
	Salt and pepper to taste
⅓	cup dark rum
	Lemon juice to taste
	Chopped hard-boiled eggs, and chopped parsley

In large kettle, cook celery, onion, parsley, thyme, and bay leaf in butter over moderately low heat, stirring for 10 minutes. Add ham hock, beans, broth, water, salt and pepper to taste. Bring to a boil, and then reduce heat, simmering uncovered for 3 hours. Add water if necessary to keep beans covered. Discard ham hock and bay leaf and purée soup in food processor. Return to kettle stir in rum, lemon juice and salt and pepper to taste. Thin soup to desired consistency with hot water. Garnish with eggs and parsley.

Smoked Bacon, Corn, and Sweet Potato Soup

6 servings

8	strips of bacon, chopped
2	large Vidalia onions, diced
2	ribs celery, diced
6	cups chicken stock
1	large sweet potato, cubed
1	(15.2-ounce) can whole kernel corn, drained
1	Knorr's chicken bouillon cube
3	tablespoons cornstarch
	Salt and pepper to taste
	Parsley
	Chopped green onions (scallions)

Cook bacon until crisp. Add onions and celery, cook until tender. Add stock and bring to a boil. Add potato, corn, bouillon, salt and pepper. Cook until potato is tender.

Stir cornstarch with enough cold water to dissolve. Whisk into the soup and cook until slightly thickened. Season with salt and pepper. Ladle into bowls and garnish with parsley, and onions.

When available, we prefer to use applewood smoked bacon.

Creamy Leek and Spinach Soup

6 servings

6	tablespoons (¾ stick) unsalted butter
1½	pounds leeks (white and pale green parts only) thinly sliced
¼	cup dry white wine
	Pinch of granulated sugar
3½	cups chicken stock or canned low-salt broth
15	ounces fresh spinach leaves, stemmed and washed
1	cup coarsely chopped fresh Italian parsley
	Dash nutmeg
½	cup whipping cream
3	tablespoons unsalted butter
	Salt and pepper to taste

Rinse leeks in water. Let the sediment settle to the bottom and lift out. Repeat if needed. Melt 3 tablespoons butter in a Dutch oven over medium heat. Add leeks; sauté until soft but not colored, about 8 minutes.

Add wine and sugar; simmer until almost all liquid evaporates, stirring occasionally, about 4 minutes. Add stock. Set aside 2 cups (packed) spinach leaves. Add remaining spinach to soup and stir until spinach wilts, about 2 minutes. Mix in parsley and nutmeg. Bring to boil. Reduce heat, cover and simmer 10 minutes to blend flavors. Working in batches, purée soup with reserved 2 cups spinach in blender. Return soup to pot. Season with salt and pepper.

Add cream and 3 tablespoons butter to soup; whisk until butter melts. Ladle into bowls.

Cranberry Cabbage Salad

After meeting Phyllis Jones the first time I knew we were friends.
She is the food service director at First Baptist Church here in Greensboro.
She has written her own cookbook, also. When we see each other we always
have a new recipe to talk about. Her mother passed this on to her and
Phyllis insisted that I try it. We have served it at church numerous
times and have yet to find someone that doesn't like this salad.

1¼ cups fresh cranberries, coarsely cut, sprinkled with 3 tablespoons sugar
4 cups broccoli florets
4 cups shredded green cabbage
1 carrot, shredded
½ cup toasted pecan pieces
½ cup raisins
⅓ cup diced red onion
6 slices bacon, cooked and crumbled

Dressing
1½ cups mayonnaise
5 teaspoons cider vinegar
6 tablespoons sugar
¾ teaspoon salt

Toss all the salad ingredients together. Whisk dressing ingredients together in a
separate bowl. Toss into salad and serve immediately.

Salad looses its crunchy texture if refrigerated overnight.

Nancy (Lipper) Pierron

Diana Tursky's "Tantalizing Tossed Salad"

Diana has been my "sous chef" on Wednesday nights when I cook at church, and a faithful assistant during furniture market catering. She is a wonderful friend and we have shared many good times together. Everyone has enjoyed our results from numerous experiments. Each time we serve this salad people request the recipe. I am proud to have Diana's creation published in our cookbook.

6 to 8 servings

Salad

	Mixed greens
4	ounces crumbled bleu cheese
1	can Mandarin oranges, drained (or sliced fresh oranges)
1	cup sliced fresh strawberries
½	small red onion, sliced
1	avocado, peeled, pitted, and sliced
6	slices cooked and crumbled bacon
2	cups cut up roasted chicken (optional)

Balsamic Vinaigrette

½	cup balsamic vinegar
1	cup olive oil
3	tablespoons Dijon mustard
3	tablespoons honey
3	tablespoons minced onion
2	garlic cloves, minced
	Salt and freshly ground pepper

Spicy Caramelized Walnuts

¼	cup granulated sugar
1	cup warm water
1	cup English walnuts
2	teaspoons chili powder (use 1 tablespoon for spicier nuts)
⅛	teaspoon ground black pepper

Salad

Mix together in a large salad bowl. Refrigerate while preparing dressing.

Diana Tursky's "Tantalizing Tossed Salad" continued

Vinaigrette

Measure ingredients into a container and shake to mix. Chill.

Walnuts

Preheat oven to 350°.

Mix together sugar, water, and walnuts and soak 10 minutes. Drain. Mix nuts with chili powder and pepper.

Bake on a buttered baking sheet 10 minutes.

Toss salad with dressing. Sprinkle nuts over the salad.

For a heartier salad add roasted chicken.

Nancy (Lipper) Pierron

Napa Cabbage Salad

We refer to Judi Bania and Kim Bobes, representatives of Kessler Industries, as our "Skinny Minis". They are conscious of every calorie of every bite they eat. They voted this salad as a low-calorie high-fiber all-you-can-eat luncheon salad.

10 to 12 Servings

Salad

1	medium head Napa cabbage, washed and shredded
2	bunches green onions, chopped
2	packages ramen noodles, crushed (discard flavor packet)
¼	cup salted butter
1	cup sliced almonds
¼	cup sesame seeds
¼	cup sunflower seeds

Dressing

¼	cup tarragon vinegar
2	tablespoons red wine vinegar
½	cup granulated sugar
¼	cup soy sauce
½	cup vegetable oil

Salad

In a salad bowl, toss the cabbage and onions together. Chill.

Sauté ramen noodles, butter, almonds, and sesame and sunflower seeds until almonds are a golden brown. Remove from heat and cool to room temperature.

Dressing

Whisk all ingredients together in a non-reactive saucepan and bring to a boil. Cook about 1 to 2 minutes. Chill and toss with the cabbage. Sprinkle the noodle-seed mixture over the cabbage and toss lightly. Serve immediately.

This salad does not keep well.

Pine Nut and Dried Cranberry Toss Salad

Larry and LeAnn Wood are members of our Agape Sunday school class.
They are also known for two of their dishes they usually bring to carry-in
dinners or other church socials. LeAnn is famous for her deviled eggs and
Larry is known for his "killer" potato salad. LeAnn especially liked
the following salad with the Poppy Seed Dressing when we served
it at another Wednesday Night Live dinner.

	A mixture of Boston, red leaf, green leaf lettuce and spinach
½	cup dried cranberries
½	cup red onion, sliced in rings
½	cup dark raisins
½	cup toasted pine nuts
1	cucumber sliced

Toss the greens together and sprinkle remaining ingredients over lettuces. Serve
with the Poppy Seed Dressing or other dressing.

Cranberry Salad

1	whole orange
1	(12-ounce) bag fresh cranberries
2	cups granulated sugar
1	tart apple, cored and cubed (Granny Smith or Jonathan)
5	ribs celery, chopped
½	cup toasted pecan pieces
2	tablespoons Grand Marnier liqueur

Begin preparing 1 day or 8 hours before serving. Remove seeds and center pith
from the orange, then purée the remaining pulp and peel in a blender. In a non-
reactive 2-quart saucepan, cook the orange purée, cranberries, and sugar until
cranberries pop and soften, about 5 minutes. Chill completely.

When ready to serve, add the cubed apple, celery, pecans and Grand Marnier.

The salad may be prepared a day in advance.

Cranberry Relish

Our Senior Minister of Mount Pisgah United Methodist Church, the Reverend Hank Thompson and his wife Marizell, have promised that the addition of their relish recipe will increase the sales of our cookbook in vast numbers! Marizell states that "the salad is very enjoyable during Thanksgiving and Christmas holidays."

1	(12-ounce) package fresh cranberries
1	large unpeeled apple, cored
1	peeled orange, seeds removed
1	unpeeled orange, seeds removed
1	cup toasted pecans
2	cups granulated sugar
1	(8-ounce) can crushed pineapple, drained

Combine the first 5 ingredients and chop in a food processor. Then mix with the pecans, sugar, and pineapple. Let stand in the refrigerator overnight before serving.

The relish will retain flavor and texture for several weeks.

Marizell Thompson

German Potato Salad for a Crowd

16 servings

Salad

5	pounds Idaho baking potatoes, boiled with skin on
8	slices bacon, cooked and drained; reserve bacon grease
2	cups chopped celery
1	red onion, sliced thin, cut in quarters
1	green bell pepper, julienne
½	red bell pepper, julienne
3	hard-boiled eggs, sliced

Dressing

⅓	cup bacon grease
⅓	cup flour
2	cups water
2	cups pure dark apple cider vinegar
¾	cup granulated sugar
1	teaspoon each salt and black pepper

Salad

In a Dutch oven cover potatoes with water and cook until fork tender. They should be firm. Let cool, peel and slice. Add celery, onion, peppers, and eggs to potatoes.

Dressing

Make a roux of the bacon fat and flour, mixing together in a 2-quart saucepan. Cook 1 minute. Stirring constantly, add water and vinegar. Bring to a boil and cook about 5 minutes. Add sugar, salt and pepper. Pour over potato-vegetable mixture, and toss lightly together to keep egg slices intact. Serve warm.

May be refrigerated, then re-warmed in the microwave.

Chicken and Wild Rice Salad

Salad

4	cups cooked wild/white rice blend
1	cup chopped celery
1	small red onion, diced
½	cup dark raisins
1	cup toasted pecan pieces
2	Granny Smith apples, cored and chopped
2	boneless chicken breasts, sautéed or grilled
	Salt and pepper to taste

Balsamic Dressing

1	cup olive oil
½	cup balsamic vinegar
¼	cup red wine vinegar
2	tablespoons Worcestershire sauce
2	tablespoons soy sauce
½	cup granulated sugar

Salad

Cook wild rice blend according to package directions. Cool slightly. Add remaining ingredients. Cut chicken into chunks and add to rice mixture.

Dressing

Whisk dressing ingredients together, and toss into chicken and rice mixture. Adjust seasonings to taste. Serve on lettuce leaf.

The salad retains flavor and texture the next day.

Vegetable Couscous Salad

1	cup chicken stock
½	teaspoon salt
¾	cup couscous
⅓	cup diced red onion
⅓	cup diced red bell pepper
1	clove garlic, minced fine
2	tablespoons red wine vinegar
¼	teaspoon ground cayenne pepper
2	tablespoons parsley
½	cup chopped fresh tomato
⅓	cup raisins or currants
½	cup sliced black olives
	Pepper to taste
	Toasted sliced almonds for garnish

Bring chicken stock and salt to boil and add couscous. Cover with a lid, remove from heat and set for 5 minutes. Fluff with a fork to separate. Add remaining ingredients and chill several hours for flavors to mellow. Sprinkle sliced almonds on top to garnish.

Grilled Pickled Shrimp with Corn Relish Salad

Shrimp Marinade

½	cup granulated sugar
1	cup orange juice
½	cup balsamic vinegar
½	cup chopped, fresh basil
½	teaspoon salt
1	large onion, sliced very thin

Salad Dressing

1	cup olive oil
2	teaspoons Old Bay seafood seasonings
2	teaspoons Dijon mustard
¼	teaspoon of hot sauce
	Salt and pepper to taste
24	jumbo peeled and deveined shrimp

Salad

1	cup snow peas
1	cup fresh, tender, young green beans
1½	cups fresh corn kernels, or canned corn, drained
¼	cup diced roasted red peppers
6	large washed lettuce leaves
	Parsley or lemon slice for garnish

Shrimp Marinade

Boil together sugar, orange juice and vinegar. Remove from heat and add basil, salt and onion. Refrigerate overnight. Remove onions from marinade. Chop and set aside.

Salad Dressing

Whisk together dressing ingredients until well combined. Stir into the marinade and reserve 1 cup of liquid. Add the chopped onions to the 1 cup of liquid and set aside to use as the dressing for the vegetables.

Add the shrimp to the marinade and chill 3 to 4 hours. Meanwhile prepare the salad.

Grilled Pickled Shrimp with Corn Relish Salad continued

Salad

Bring water to boil in a large pot. Add peas and beans; cook 2 to 3 minutes. Drain and plunge into ice water to stop the cooking process. Drain.

Marinate vegetables in a separate bowl. Toss together the cooled beans, peas, fresh or canned corn, and red peppers. Add the 1 cup of dressing with reserved chopped onion.

Remove shrimp from marinade and grill or cook in a hot, dry skillet, about 2 minutes on each side, until pink.

Arrange lettuce leaf on a plate; spoon a portion of vegetables in the center of each leaf. Arrange shrimp on top of salad. Garnish with parsley leaf and lemon slice, if desired.

Cece's Coleslaw

Our cousin Cece (Harris) Long acquired this coleslaw recipe in
1985 from a former college roommate. It is a zippy, cool,
summer salad, something different at an outdoor BBQ.

8	cups thin shredded green cabbage
2	carrots, grated
1	small green bell pepper, diced
1	small yellow onion, diced
2	tablespoons mustard seed
⅓	cup vegetable oil

Dressing
½	cup cider vinegar
1	cup granulated sugar
⅓	cup water
1	teaspoon salt
1	(3-ounce) box lemon flavored gelatin

Slaw

Mix all ingredients together. Chill while preparing dressing.

Dressing

Bring vinegar, sugar, water, and salt to a boil. Pour over gelatin to dissolve. Cool, then pour over cabbage mixture and toss to mix. Chill overnight.

Cece has not tried this, but says the salad can be frozen and used at a later date.

Jicama and Pineapple Salad

Dressing

⅓	cup vegetable oil
3	tablespoons white wine vinegar
1	tablespoon minced shallots
¼	cup minced, fresh cilantro
¼	teaspoon ground cumin
2	tablespoons granulated sugar
6	ounces fresh baby spinach, washed and stems trimmed
1	small jicama, peeled and cut into 3-inch-long match-stick size strips
1	cup cubed fresh pineapple

Whisk together oil, vinegar, shallots, cilantro, cumin, and sugar.

Toss with the spinach, jicama, and pineapple.

Serve immediately.

Sliced red onion and Mandarin orange segments may be added.

Fresh Frozen Fruit

Our mother, Marilee Lipper, found a thrifty way to preserve fresh fruit
for the cold winter months. It is perfect for a last minute dinner salad.
Thaw a container of fruit to ease summer fruit cravings.

Syrup

4	cups granulated sugar
8	cups water
1	(6-ounce) can orange juice concentrate
1	(6-ounce) can lemonade concentrate

Fruit

2	cantaloupes, cubed or balled
1	honeydew melon, cubed or balled
1	small watermelon, cubed or balled
1½	pounds seedless green grapes
1½	pounds red seedless grapes
3	pounds fresh peeled, sliced peaches
1	pound fresh blueberries

Syrup

Bring sugar and water to boil, then add orange juice and lemonade. Continue to
boil 5 minutes longer. Remove from heat.

Fruit

Remove seeds from the cantaloupe and honeydew, and as many seeds as possible
from the watermelon. In a large bowl combine the fruit and divide into the mixed
fruit in serving size containers. Pour hot syrup over the fruit, leaving a 1-inch top
space. Cover with a lid and freeze. Thaw and serve in fruit cups.

Fresh sliced bananas or fresh strawberries may be added when ready to serve.

Pesto Pecan Basil Dressing

2 quarts

¼   teaspoon salt
2   teaspoons Dijon mustard
2   cloves garlic
1   tablespoon granulated sugar
1   egg
1   egg yolk
3   tablespoons fresh lemon juice
2   tablespoons honey
¼   cup red wine vinegar
2   cups (approximately) vegetable or olive oil
4   ounces fresh basil leaves
¾   cup toasted pecan pieces

In a food processor purée first 9 ingredients. Slowly drizzle in oil to emulsify. Pour into a container. In the processor chop onion with basil leaves. Add the pecans and pulse lightly. Stir into dressing base.

The dressing amount may need to be separated into 2 batches to fit in the processor bowl. The amount of oil used depends upon each individual taste. Less oil used results in a tangy dressing.

Freshly prepared dressing keeps 2 to 3 weeks in the refrigerator.

Poppyseed Dressing

1 quart

1	cup granulated sugar
1	tablespoon dry yellow mustard
1	tablespoon salt
1	cup red wine vinegar
½	red onion, chopped (approximately 1 cup)
3	cups vegetable oil
1	tablespoon poppy seeds

Measure sugar, mustard, salt, vinegar, and onion into food processor. Puree until smooth. Slowly pour oil through the food tube and process until thick and pink.

Serve over any salad combination or fresh fruit.

Creamy Curry Dressing

1¼ cups

1	cup mayonnaise
¼	cup sour cream
1	teaspoon minced onion
1	garlic clove, minced
1¼	teaspoons curry powder
	Pinch of cumin
	Pinch of cayenne pepper
	Pinch of caraway seed
	Pinch of fennel seed

Mix the mayonnaise, sour cream, onion, garlic, curry powder, cumin, and cayenne pepper. With a mallet crush the caraway and fennel seeds. Stir into the dressing. Refrigerate 24 hours before serving to allow flavors to mellow.

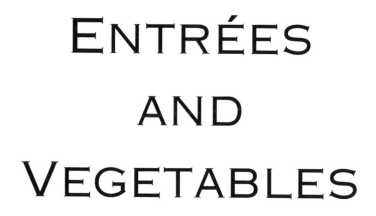

ENTRÉES
AND
VEGETABLES

Chicken Tetrazzini

6 to 8 servings

8	ounces thin spaghetti
1	cup sliced fresh mushrooms
2	tablespoons unsalted butter
1	(10½-ounce) can cream of mushroom soup
1	(10½-ounce) can cream of celery soup
1	cup half-and-half
1	cup white wine
½	cup diced red bell peppers
½	cup diced green bell peppers
½	cup diced yellow onions
¼	cup minced fresh parsley
1	tablespoon minced fresh garlic
	Salt and black pepper to taste
2	cups cooked pulled chicken
2	cups shredded Cheddar cheese
	Parmesan cheese to sprinkle on top

Preheat oven to 350°. Butter a 9x13-inch baking pan, or a 3-quart baking dish.

Break spaghetti in half and cook according to package directions. Drain.

Sauté mushrooms in butter until soft.

Stir together the soups, half-and-half, and wine. Add remaining ingredients and toss in spaghetti. Transfer to baking pan and sprinkle with Parmesan cheese.

Bake 30 minutes until edges and center are bubbly.

Chicken Pot Pie

8 to 10 servings

1	(3-pound) chicken
3	cups water
2	bay leaves
1	teaspoon salt
1	large onion chopped
1	cup chopped celery
3	carrots, peeled and sliced
3	Idaho potatoes, peeled and cubed
3	tablespoons cornstarch
½	cup cold water
1	cup frozen green peas
½	teaspoon poultry seasoning
	Salt and pepper to taste
1	chicken bouillon cube
½	cup heavy cream
	Pie crust to fit a 10-inch deep-dish pie pan.

Preheat oven to 400°.

In a 5-quart Dutch oven, cook chicken with giblets in water with bay leaves and salt. Simmer 35 minutes. Remove chicken and giblets and strain broth into a container.

De-bone chicken and cube while vegetables are cooking. Return broth to Dutch oven. Bring to a boil and add onion, celery, carrots, and potatoes. Cook potatoes al dente. Dissolve the cornstarch in water and whisk into the broth. Add the frozen peas, poultry seasoning, salt and pepper, chicken bouillon, and cream. Remove from heat. Add the cubed chicken and ladle into the crust-lined pie pan. Cover with the top crust and bake 35 to 40 minutes until crust is brown and juices bubble.

Chicken and Sausage, and Shrimp Jambalaya

12 servings

1	(3-pound) chicken
1	celery rib with leaves
1	onion, halved skin on
2	cloves garlic
2	cups converted long-grain rice
1	pound smoked andouille sausage, sliced into ½-inch pieces
1	pound ham, cured
4	tablespoons unsalted butter
1	cup chopped onion
3	ribs celery, chopped
¾	cup chopped green pepper
4	cloves garlic, minced
1	(16-ounce) can diced tomatoes
1	(6-ounce) can tomato paste
2	bay leaves
¼	teaspoon thyme
	Salt and pepper to taste
¼	teaspoon hot sauce, or to taste
4	tablespoons minced fresh parsley
1	pound raw shrimp, peeled and deveined

In a 5-quart Dutch oven, cover chicken with water. Add celery, onion, and garlic; boil until tender, about 1 hour. Strain and reserve stock. Remove meat from bones. Set aside.

In a 4-quart saucepan cook rice in 4 cups of the chicken stock, 15 minutes.

In a Dutch oven, fry sausage and ham until lightly browned, about 3 to 5 minutes. Remove meat. Add butter to pan and sauté onion, celery, pepper, and garlic 3 minutes over low heat. Stir in tomatoes, tomato paste, bay leaves, thyme, salt and pepper, and hot sauce. Simmer 20 minutes. Add sausage, ham, and raw shrimp. Cook 5 minutes, until shrimp is done. Sprinkle with parsley.

Spoon rice onto a serving plate and ladle Jambalaya over rice.

Smoked Sausage Cassoulet

8 to 10 servings

2	tablespoons olive oil
3	pounds smoked Kielbasa and Andouille sausage
4	large leeks (white and pale green parts only)
6	garlic cloves, minced.
1	medium golden delicious apple, peeled and sliced
1	tablespoon minced fresh rosemary
1½	teaspoons dried rubbed sage
½	cup brandy
2	(14½-ounce) cans diced roasted garlic tomatoes
3	(15-ounce) cans Great Northern beans, drained
1	(10-ounce) package frozen baby lima beans
1½	cups chicken broth
3	tablespoons tomato paste
½	teaspoon ground cloves
	Salt and pepper
¼	cup olive oil
4	cups diced French bread
1	pound fresh tomatoes, seeded and diced
½	cup minced fresh parsley

Preheat oven to 350°.

In an ovenproof roasting pan heat 2 tablespoons oil over medium heat. Add sausages; sauté until brown, about 20 minutes. Transfer to a plate and cut into ½-inch pieces.

Slice leeks into thin rounds and place in a pot of water to rinse. Let the sediment settle to the bottom and lift leeks from water and drain. Repeat rinsing if needed. Into the roasting pan add leeks and garlic and sauté until soften. Mix in apple, rosemary, and sage. Add brandy and simmer until almost evaporated, about 5 minutes. Stir in canned tomatoes with juices, canned beans, lima beans, chicken broth, tomato paste, and cloves. Add sausages. Season with salt and pepper.

Bring cassoulet to boil. Cover pot and bake in oven 30 minutes.

Heat ¼ cup olive oil in a large skillet over medium heat. Add bread and sauté until golden brown, stirring constantly, about 25 minutes. Combine fresh tomatoes and parsley in a large bowl and mix in bread. Season topping with salt and pepper. Spoon onto hot cassoulet. Bake uncovered 15 minutes longer.

Roasted Pork Loin Stuffed with Dried Fruit

10 to 12 servings

5	pound boneless pork loin, trimmed of fat
2	Granny Smith apples; peeled, cored, and sliced
½	cup unsalted butter
3	garlic cloves, minced
1	cup chopped onion
½	cup chopped celery
½	cup dried cranberries
1	cup dried prunes, cut in half
1	cup dried figs, cut in half
½	cup dried apricots, cut in half
½	cup apricot or fig preserves
2	tablespoons orange liqueur
½	cup toasted pecans

Preheat oven to 350°.

In a large pan sauté butter, garlic, onion, and celery until tender. Add the cranberries, prunes, figs, apricots, preserves liqueur, and pecans. Remove from heat; cool slightly.

To make a hole for the stuffing that runs through the center of the loin, begin in the middle of the cut edge and with a long thin knife make an incision toward the center. Repeat the procedure starting on the opposite end. With the handle of a wooden spoon stretch the opening wider and fill the cavity from both ends with the stuffing. Season the outside generously with salt and pepper. Place in a roasting pan and bake loin, covered with aluminum foil, for 45 minutes to an hour until internal temperature reaches 160° on a meat thermometer.

Remove pork from roasting pan and deglaze pan with water. Scrape down brown bits. Boil au jus to reduce by ½ and strain. Serve au jus as an accompaniment.

Slice pork in ¾-inch servings.

Spicy Southwest Beef and Bell Pepper Stew

6 servings

Seasoning

1	tablespoon ground cumin
2½	teaspoons ground coriander
2½	teaspoons chili powder
2	teaspoons dried oregano, crumbled
2	teaspoons dried thyme
¼	teaspoon ground cloves
¼	teaspoon ground allspice
¼	teaspoon ground cinnamon

Mix all ingredients in a container. Set aside.

Stew

1	cup dried pinto beans, rinsed, and sorted
1	(3-pound) boneless chuck roast, trimmed and cut into 1-inch cubes
	Salt and pepper
	Seasoning mix, divided
3	tablespoons all-purpose flour
6	tablespoons vegetable oil
2	large onions, cut into ½-inch pieces
8	garlic cloves, minced
1	jalapeño chili, minced with seeds
3	tablespoons tomato paste
1½	cups red Zinfandel wine
2	cups beef stock or canned broth
2	cups chicken broth or canned broth
1	(28-ounce) can plum tomatoes, drained
1	smoked ham hock
½	teaspoon dried red pepper flakes
11	ounces smoked kielbasa sausage, cut diagonally into 1-inch pieces
2	red or yellow bell peppers, cut into 1½-inch pieces
2	poblano chilies, cut into 1½-inch pieces
3	zucchini, cut into 1-inch-thick rounds
	Minced fresh cilantro

Spicy Southwest Beef and Bell Pepper Stew continued

Place beans in a 4-quart saucepan with enough cold water to cover. Bring to a boil. Remove from heat. Cover and let stand 1 hour. Strain and set aside.

Place beef in a large bowl. Sprinkle with 2 teaspoons seasoning mix and toss well.

Heat 4 tablespoons oil in a heavy 4-quart Dutch oven over medium heat. Sear meat, in batches browning well. Using a slotted spoon transfer to a bowl.

Heat remaining 2 tablespoons oil to the same pan. Reduce heat to medium. Add onion and all but 2 teaspoons remaining seasoning mix and toss to coat. Stir in garlic, jalapeño and tomato paste. Add wine and bring to boil, scraping up browned bits. Add stocks, tomatoes, ham hock and red pepper flakes and bring to a simmer. Return meat to Dutch oven. Reduce heat, cover and simmer 30 minutes, stirring occasionally. Add beans, cover and simmer 1 hour. Uncover, add reserved 2 teaspoons seasoning mix and simmer until meat and beans are tender, stirring occasionally, about 45 minutes.

Skim fat from stew if necessary. Remove ham hock, trim fat and discard. Cut ham meat into ½-inch pieces. Return to stew.

Cook Kielbasa sausage in a heavy skillet until cooked through, about 2 minutes per side. Transfer to a plate. Add peppers, poblano chilies and zucchini and sauté until crisp-tender, about 5 minutes. Mix sausage and vegetables into stew and simmer until just tender, about 5 minutes longer. Sprinkle with cilantro.

Ladle into bowls, and serve with crusty bread.

Seared Pork Tenderloin with Bell Pepper Chutney

10 servings

2	pork tenderloins, trimmed
1	tablespoon butter
2	teaspoons minced fresh garlic
1	teaspoon minced fresh gingerroot
1	small minced jalapeño pepper, seeded
1	cup diced red bell pepper
1	cup diced yellow bell pepper
1	cup diced Vidalia onion, or yellow onion
1	cup Major Grey's Chutney
¼	cup golden raisins
¼	teaspoon salt
	Dash of ground black pepper
	Dash of ground cumin

Preheat oven to 400°. Season tenderloins with salt and pepper. In an ovenproof pan sear the tenderloins in olive oil and garlic, browning on all sides. Place tenderloins in the oven for 15 minutes.

In a sauté pan over medium heat cook butter, garlic, gingerroot, jalapeño pepper, red pepper, yellow pepper, and onion until soft and tender. Add the chutney, raisins, salt, pepper, and cumin. Cook 4 minutes longer on low heat.

Pork-E-Pine Balls

"This recipe was handed down from my husband's grandmother. When my sister-in-law from New Jersey came to visit we told her we were having Pork-E-Pines for dinner and she was very hesitant to take the first bite at our Southern table!"

4 servings

"Pine" balls

1	pound ground beef
¾	cup instant rice
¼	cup diced onion
½	teaspoon salt
	Dash of black pepper

Sauce

2	tablespoons oil
½	cup chopped celery
¼	cup diced onion
2	(10¾-ounce) cans tomato soup
⅔	cup water
¼	cup fresh lemon juice
1	teaspoon Worcestershire sauce
¼	cup packed light brown sugar
2	teaspoons dry mustard
1	teaspoon salt
¼	teaspoon black pepper

"Pine" balls

Mix meatball ingredients together and roll into an egg shape using a tablespoon to shape. Refrigerate until ready to use.

Sauce

Combine ingredients for the sauce in a Dutch oven or large skillet. Drop pines into the sauce and simmer very slowly on low heat, about 20 minutes or put in the oven a 350° for 1 hour. Serve with rice.

The longer you simmer the sauce the better the flavor.

Pines and sauce can be made ahead and frozen separately for cooking later.

Megan Cohan

Marinated Grilled Veal Chops with Vidalia Onion Compote (Cover Photo)

The unique soil and climate conditions are the key to growing true Vidalia onions in and around the area of Vidalia, Georgia. Harvested in spring, the mild sweet onions are shipped worldwide, and are coveted by chefs near and far. When caramelized Vidalia onions have a sweeter flavor than most onions.

My former neighbors, Rusty and Wendy Phillips shared the following recipe with me. On several different occasions we tested and critiqued each other's creations. We have yet to find BBQ and smoked turkey better than what Rusty prepares.

8 servings

Marinade

2	garlic cloves, minced
⅓	cup balsamic vinegar
½	cup olive oil
⅓	cup white wine
1	sprig of fresh rosemary
1	sprig of fresh thyme
	Salt and pepper to taste
8	veal chops

Compote

4	ounces bacon, cut into small pieces
8	ounces Vidalia onions, chopped
2	tablespoons granulated sugar
2	tablespoons water
¼	cup sherry vinegar

Marinade

Combine the marinade ingredients in a shallow dish. Add the veal chops and refrigerate 2 to 4 hours, turning once.

Preheat grill, and grill the veal chops until done to taste.

Compote

Preheat oven to 350°. Cook the bacon in a skillet over high heat until nearly crisp. Drain. Add the onions and sauté until the onions are tender.

Combine the sugar and water in a heavy saucepan. Cook until the mixture begins to caramelize. Add the vinegar. Cook until reduced by half. Add the onion and

Marinated Grilled Veal Chops with Vidalia Onion Compote continued

bacon mixture. Bring to a boil and spoon into a baking dish. Lay parchment paper over the dish and bake 20 minutes.

Serve over the grilled veal chops.

Covering the dish with parchment paper instead of aluminum foil prevents extra moisture from forming in the compote.

Nancy (Lipper) Pierron

Korean Beef Kabobs
8 servings

10	green onions with tops
3	garlic cloves, minced
¼	cup soy sauce
½	teaspoon salt
¼	cup sesame seeds
½	teaspoon ground black pepper
3	tablespoons sesame oil
3	tablespoons vegetable oil
2	tablespoons honey
2	tablespoon granulated sugar
2	pounds sirloin tip or sirloin steak
1	pint cherry tomatoes
1	(16-ounce) can pineapple chunks
1	green bell pepper, cut in 1-inch pieces
1	red bell pepper, cut in 1-inch pieces
1	red onion, cut into wedges, or 6-ounces shallots
1	(8-ounce) package whole mushrooms

Mix first 10 ingredients in a bowl. Cut sirloin into 2-inch cubes. Coat in the marinade and refrigerate 2 to 4 hours.

Preheat grill. Skewer vegetables alternately with meat and place on grill for 8 to 10 minutes, turning and basting with remaining marinade while grilling.

Wild Rice Pilaf with Carrots and Fennel

6 servings

2	medium fennel bulbs, tough outer layer discarded, trimmed, halved and cored
10	tablespoons unsalted butter
4	carrots, peeled and julienne (match-stick)
1	cup chopped onion
1	teaspoon dried thyme
1	teaspoon dried crumbled tarragon
1	teaspoon salt
4	cups beef stock
1	cup dry white wine
2½	cups converted wild/white rice blend
	Minced fresh parsley

Dice fennel into ¼-inch pieces. Heat butter in a heavy Dutch oven over medium and add fennel and carrots; cook 4 minutes. Add onion and cook 3 minutes Mix in thyme, tarragon, and salt.

Bring the stock and wine to a boil. Add rice blend and reduce heat to the lowest temperature. Cover and cook until rice is just tender and all liquid is absorbed, about 20 minutes. Add vegetable mixture to rice and toss together. Serve, sprinkled with parsley.

Minnie Beasley-Wright's
Favorite Hash Brown Casserole

Minnie is the Customer Service Manager at Kessler Industries of El Paso, Texas.
We met her during furniture market in High Point, North Carolina
when we catered for Kessler Industries. Since she is a vegetarian,
we revised the recipe to make it a complete vegetarian dish.
We received high marks each morning it was served.

It is easy to prepare, refrigerates well, and is delicious reheated.

10 servings

2	pounds (4 cups) frozen shredded hash browns
½	cup chopped celery
½	cup chopped onion
½	cup chopped green bell pepper
2	teaspoons salt
1	teaspoon ground black pepper
1	cup sour cream
1	cup ranch dressing
2	cups grated Cheddar cheese
1	can cream of celery soup
½	cup unsalted butter, melted
2	cups crushed cornflakes
¼	cup melted unsalted butter

Preheat oven to 350°. Butter a 9x13-inch pan.

Mix all ingredients, except the cornflakes and ¼ cup butter, in a large bowl. Spread
in the prepared pan. Toss the cornflakes and ¼ cup butter together and sprinkle
over the hash browns. Bake 45 to 50 minutes until bubbling around edges and in
the center.

Measure cornflakes after they have been crushed.

Sweet Potato Balls

8 servings

4	cups cooked, cold mashed sweet potatoes
¾	cup miniature marshmallows
¼	cup unsalted butter, melted
½	teaspoon salt
¼	teaspoon ground black pepper

⅓	cup honey
1½	cups chopped pecans
¼	cup unsalted butter, melted

Combine the sweet potatoes, marshmallows, butter, salt, and pepper. Shape into individual balls. Place on a sheet pan; cover and refrigerate overnight.

Preheat oven to 350°. Butter a 9x13-inch baking pan.

In the microwave heat honey to liquefy. Roll each ball in the honey, then in the pecans. Place in the prepared pan and drizzle with the ¼ cup butter. Bake 30 minutes to heat through.

Potatoes will be fragile and soft to serve.

White and Sweet Potato Au Gratin

A colorful and easy accompaniment to any entrée.

2	Idaho baking potatoes, peeled and sliced
2	sweet potatoes, peeled and sliced
1	Vidalia or yellow onion, peeled and sliced
4	garlic cloves, minced
¼	cup grated Parmesan cheese
2	teaspoons salt
1	teaspoon ground white pepper
1½	cups heavy cream

Preheat oven to 350°. Generously butter a 9x13-inch baking pan or a 10-inch quiche pan.

Layer potatoes alternately with the onion. Sprinkle garlic, cheese, and salt and pepper over potatoes. Pour cream over entire surface and bake 45 to 50 minutes, basting occasionally. Potatoes will be golden brown and bubbly around edges.

Sweet Potato Soufflé

We have added this soufflé to our traditional holiday menu.
As a side accompaniment it could be confused as a dessert.

12 servings

Soufflé

3	cups cooked mashed sweet potatoes
½	cup packed light brown sugar
2	eggs
1	teaspoon vanilla
½	cup evaporated milk or half-and-half
½	cup salted butter
½	teaspoon salt
1	teaspoon ground cinnamon
¼	teaspoon ground ginger

Topping

1	cup pecan pieces
¾	cup packed brown sugar
¼	cup all-purpose flour
¼	cup melted salted butter
¾	teaspoon ground cinnamon
	Dash of ground cloves

Soufflé

Preheat oven to 350°. Butter a 9x13-inch pan or a soufflé dish.

Mix hot potatoes with the sugar, eggs, and vanilla. Stir in the milk or half-and-half, butter salt, cinnamon, and ginger. Spread in the prepared pan and sprinkle with the Topping.

Topping

Blend all ingredients to a moist crumb mixture. Sprinkle over the soufflé mixture and bake 25 to 30 minutes. Topping will be crisp and browned.

The flavor is better reheated the next day.

Brussels Sprouts, Apples, and Chestnuts

4	ounces fresh chestnuts
8	ounces Brussels sprouts
1	tart apple, peeled cored, and sliced
1	small yellow onion
¼	cup unsalted butter
3	tablespoons Dijon mustard
½	cup sour cream
2	tablespoons honey
	Salt and white pepper to taste

With a sharp pointed knife, cut an X in the skin of each chestnut. Cover with water and boil 20 minutes. While hot, remove peel and inner hull. Trim any dark spots off the nut meat. Set aside.

Trim and cut off stem ends of the Brussels sprouts. Cook in salted boiling water 5 minutes until almost tender, but still bright green. Drain and set aside.

Slice onion and apple and sauté in butter until tender. Add mustard, sour cream, and honey. Toss in Brussels sprouts, and chestnuts. Heat over medium heat just to warm. Season with salt and pepper.

Corn and Sour Cream Bake

For one Wednesday Night Live this was a throw together of ingredients
available at church. It was well received, especially by Don Cohan.
He came back for seconds and even thirds. He insisted I write out
a recipe and has frequently asked if it was going to be in the cookbook.
Here is the final draft after many modifications.

8 servings

8	slices bacon
2	tablespoons unsalted butter
1	medium Vidalia or yellow onion, minced
¼	cup diced red bell pepper
¼	cup diced green bell pepper
1	celery rib, diced
1	cup sliced fresh mushrooms
1	cup sour cream
2	tablespoons all-purpose flour
¼	cup granulated sugar
2	tablespoons minced fresh parsley
1	teaspoon salt
1	teaspoon ground white pepper
2	(15.2-ounce) cans whole kernel corn drained, or 16 ounces frozen corn

Preheat oven to 350°. Butter a 2-quart baking dish.

Cook bacon until crisp. Remove from pan, but do not drain the fat. In the same
pan add the butter and sauté the onion, peppers, celery, and mushrooms until
tender. Remove from heat.

In a mixing bowl stir the sour cream, flour, sugar, parsley, salt, and pepper together.
Crumble the bacon and mix in with the corn and cooked vegetables. Pour into the
prepared pan and bake 35 to 40 minutes until edges are bubbly.

Nancy (Lipper) Pierron

Zucchini-Corn Pudding

8 to 10 servings

¼	cup unsalted butter
¼	cup olive oil
½	cup minced yellow onion
½	cup diced green bell pepper
2	garlic cloves, minced
2	pounds unpeeled zucchini, cubed
2	cups canned or frozen corn
1	teaspoon salt
1	teaspoon ground black pepper
¾	teaspoon ground cayenne pepper
3	egg yolks
1	cup grated Cheddar cheese
1	cup unsalted butter, melted
3	tablespoons granulated sugar
3	egg whites

Preheat oven to 350°. Butter a 1½-quart baking dish.

In a large pan, sauté butter and oil with onion, pepper, garlic, and zucchini for 5 to 8 minutes. Drain canned corn and add with seasonings. Remove from heat and cool.

Add yolks, cheese, melted butter, and sugar. With the wire whip attachment on an electric mixture whip whites and fold into the cooled vegetable mixture. Pour into prepared pan and place in a pan of hot water. Bake 1 hour. Serve while hot.

Pudding may be baked ahead and reheated.

Zucchini and Tomato Bake

8 to 10 servings

¼	cup unsalted butter
2	tablespoons olive oil
4	garlic cloves, minced
1	large yellow onion, sliced
5	medium zucchini, sliced ¼-inch thick
2	green bell peppers, diced
	Salt and pepper to taste
1	cup grated mozzarella cheese
1	(28-ounce) can diced tomatoes
¼	cup chopped fresh basil
2	tablespoons all-purpose flour
3	tablespoons packed light brown sugar
	Grated Parmesan cheese
	Italian breadcrumbs (optional)

Preheat oven to 350°. Butter a 9x13-inch pan.

In a large skillet heat butter and olive oil and sauté with the garlic, onions, zucchini, and peppers, until soft. Season with salt and pepper. Spread in the prepared pan. Set aside.

In the same pan mix together the tomatoes, basil, flour, and brown sugar. Heat until bubbly, pour over the zucchini layer. Sprinkle with Parmesan cheese and cover with the breadcrumbs. Bake 35 minutes until heated through and bubbly. Serve hot.

Black Bean, Corn, and Cilantro Salad

12 servings

Salad

¼	cup diced red onion
½	bunch diced green onion
2	tablespoons olive oil
2	tablespoons chopped fresh cilantro
½	green bell pepper, diced
2	jalapeño peppers, minced
2	tablespoons cider vinegar
1	tablespoon balsamic vinegar
2	teaspoons ground cumin
¼	teaspoon hot sauce
	Salt and pepper to taste
2	(15½-ounce) cans black beans, drained and rinsed
1	(15¼-ounce) can whole kernel corn, drained
1	large ripe tomato, de-seeded and diced

Yellow Rice

1	cup converted white rice
1	teaspoon olive oil
2	cups water
½	teaspoon turmeric
1	teaspoon salt

2	grilled or sautéed chicken breasts
	Black olives
	Sour cream
	Sliced avocado
	Diced fresh tomato
	Tomato Basil tortillas or flour tortillas
	Vegetable oil for frying

Salad

Toss the salad ingredients together in a bowl. Chill 8 hours or overnight to mellow flavors.

Black Bean, Corn, and Cilantro Salad continued

Yellow Rice

Blend rice, oil, water, turmeric, and salt in a 2-quart saucepan. Bring to a boil, reduce heat and cook 15 minutes. Cool.

In a shallow pan heat 2 inches of oil. Cut tortillas into triangles and fry on low heat to a golden brown. Drain on a paper towel and sprinkle with salt.

Assembly: Arrange rice onto a platter. Ladle salad over rice and garnish with chicken strips, black olives, sour cream, avocado, and tomato. For a dramatic presentation stand tortilla triangles upright in the salad or serve on the side in a basket.

Fresh Tomato Tart

8 servings

	Pastry shell to fit an 11-inch tart pan
1	egg yolk
¼	cup Dijon mustard
3	pounds fresh tomatoes
1	small yellow onion, sliced
¼	cup coarse chopped fresh basil
½	yellow bell pepper, julienne
2	ounces mozzarella cheese, crumbled
2	ounces grated Parmesan cheese
1	teaspoon salt
	White pepper to taste
½	cup black olives, sliced (optional)
2	tablespoons olive oil

Freeze unbaked shell before baking. Preheat oven to 425°.

Fit a piece of parchment paper over the unbaked shell and fill with dry beans or rice. This prevents crust from shrinking when baked. Place shell in the oven and prebake 10 minutes. Remove the beans or rice and parchment paper. Brush crust with the egg yolk. Return to the oven and bake just to dry the yolk, about 3 minutes. Remove and lower the oven temperature to 375°.

Peel, de-seed, and slice tomatoes. Drain. Brush the baked shell with the mustard. Place a layer of tomatoes over the mustard. Sprinkle with salt and pepper and ½ of the onions, basil, and yellow pepper. Layer with the remaining tomatoes and cover with remaining onions, basil, and yellow pepper. Cover top with the cheese and olives. Drizzle with olive oil and bake 20 minutes.

Brushing the crust with the yolk hinders the crust from becoming soggy from the vegetable juices. Fresh vine-ripened seasonal tomatoes are best in this tart.

EGG BRUNCH CASSEROLE *p.36* WITH
MAPLE PECAN SCONE *p.34*

PINE NUT AND DRIED
CRANBERRY TOSS SALAD *p.53*

SMOKED BACON, CORN, AND
SWEET POTATO SOUP *p.47*

ZUCCHINI AND TOMATO BAKE *p.85*

WHITE & SWEET
POTATO AU GRATIN *p.80*

SEARED PORK TENDERLOIN
WITH BELL PEPPER CHUTNEY *p.74*

RASPBERRY
MERINGUE
TORTE *p.94*

CHOCOLATE MOUSSE TORTE *p.110*

PRALINES *p.141*

SHORTBREAD *p.129*

CHOCOLATE MACAROON BROWNIES
p.137

CANDIED FRUIT SLICES *p.126*

DESIGNER CAKES AND ELEGANT DESSERTS

Strawberry-Mascarpone Trifle

10 to 12 servings

3   quarts fresh strawberries, stemmed and sliced lengthwise into ¼ inch pieces; reserve 6 to 10 whole unstemmed berries for garnish

2   tablespoons orange liqueur

6   tablespoons granulated sugar, divided

3   cups heavy cream

1   cup mascarpone cheese

1   teaspoon vanilla

2   eggs

2   egg yolks

½   cup granulated sugar

1   cup cake flour

½   teaspoon salt

Combine the sliced strawberries, orange liqueur, and 2 tablespoons sugar. Toss to mix, and chill until ready to assemble dessert.

In another bowl fitted with the whip attachment whip cream, 4 tablespoons sugar, mascarpone cheese, and vanilla to soft peaks. Cover and chill.

Preheat oven to 350°. Line 2 (8-inch) round cake pans with parchment paper.

In a mixing bowl over a pan of hot, not boiling, water, whip eggs, yolks, and remaining ½ cup sugar until pale yellow and fluffy, 5 to 6 minutes. Transfer bowl to mixer and whip on high speed until light and tripled in volume, 5 minutes more. Sift cake flour and salt and fold into egg mixture in three parts. Pour batter into pans and bake until tops are golden and springs back when touched, 15 to 18 minutes. Cool to room temperature.

With a serrated knife, trim sides to fit into trifle bowl if needed. Drizzle cake layers with the juice from the macerated strawberries.

Layer from the bottom: stawberries, cream, and cake. Repeat layering process. Top trifle with cream and garnish with the reserved whole strawberries. Chill until ready to serve.

Fresh raspberries, blueberries, and blackberries are other suggestions for a mixed fruit trifle.

Coconut Layer Cake

We served this cake numerous times when we owned
Le Petit Cafe in Columbia, Missouri.

Kay Bonnetti, a good friend, customer, and loyal supporter,
loved this cake served with raspberry sauce. Kay had an organic garden
and supplied us with fresh herbs and produce during the summer.

16 to 18 servings

Cake

1	large egg
5	large egg whites
¾	cup cream of coconut
¼	cup water
1	teaspoon vanilla extract
1	teaspoon coconut extract
2¼	cups cake flour
1	cup granulated sugar
1	tablespoon baking powder
¾	teaspoon salt
12	tablespoons unsalted butter, at room temperature
2	cups flaked coconut

Custard Filling

¾	cup cream of coconut, then fill measuring cup with milk to 1⅓ cups
½	cup granulated sugar
⅓	cup all-purpose flour
¼	teaspoon salt
2	egg yolks
1	teaspoon vanilla

Butter Cream

2	large egg whites
½	cup granulated sugar
	Dash of salt
1	cup unsalted butter, cut into 1 inch pieces, at room temperature
	remaining cream of coconut
½	teaspoon coconut extract
1	teaspoon vanilla extract

Coconut Layer Cake continued

Cake

Preheat oven to 350°. Line 3 (9-inch) round cake pans with parchment paper.

Whisk egg whites and whole egg in a bowl to combine. Add cream of coconut, water, vanilla, and coconut extract and stir to combine.

Sift flour, sugar, baking powder, and salt into a mixing bowl of an electric mixer fitted with the paddle attachment. With mixer on lowest speed add butter slowly and beat until mixture resembles coarse meal, 2 to 3 minutes. Add 1 cup of the liquid. Increase speed to medium-high and beat until light and fluffy, about 1 minute. On low speed add remaining liquid to thoroughly incorporate. Batter will be thick.

Divide batter between the 3 prepared pans and spread to smooth tops. Bake until golden brown and tester inserted in the center comes out clean, about 25 to 30 minutes. Cool in pans before assembling,

Custard Filling

Combine the coconut and milk, sugar, flour, and salt in a heavy bottomed 2-quart saucepan. Bring to a boil, stirring constantly until thick. Remove from heat. Beat yolks and vanilla slightly in a small bowl. Add some of the hot mixture and whisk well. Whisk back into the saucepan. Return to low heat and cook until mixture boils, stirring constantly. Remove from heat, cover and chill 4 hours until completely cold.

Butter Cream

Combine whites, sugar, and salt in a bowl of an electric mixer. Set bowl over a saucepan of barely simmering water. Stir constantly until mixture is warm to the touch, about 3 minutes. Transfer bowl to mixer and with the whip attachment whip whites on high speed until glossy and barely warm to the touch, about 7 minutes. Whip in butter 1 piece at a time. The whites will deflate, but emulsify when all the butter is added. Whip in cream of coconut and coconut and vanilla extracts.

To assemble cake, spread ½ of the custard on one cake layer and stack with the second layer. Spread on remaining custard and stack with third layer. Coat cake with butter cream and cover with coconut. Chill until ready to serve.

Cream of coconut is found in the juice aisle or the mixed drink aisle of any grocery store.

Raspberry Meringue Torte

12 to 16 servings

Sponge Cake

3	eggs
3	egg yolks
⅓	cup granulated sugar
1	teaspoon vanilla
½	teaspoon salt
¾	cup cake flour
¾	teaspoon baking powder
2	tablespoons unsalted butter
¼	cup milk
1	cup of your favorite vanilla butter cream
2	pints fresh raspberries

Meringue

6	egg whites
¼	teaspoon cream of tartar
½	cup granulated sugar
	pinch of salt
1	teaspoon vanilla

Sponge Cake

Preheat oven to 350°. Line 3 (8-inch) round cake pans with parchment paper.

Sift together flour, baking powder, and salt.

Combine the eggs, yolks, sugar, and vanilla in the bowl of a standing mixer and place over a pan of hot, not boiling water, stirring constantly until mixture is warm to the touch. Using the whip attachment on the mixer, whip egg mixture until pale and tripled in volume, about 5 minutes. While eggs are whipping heat butter and milk until butter melts; keep hot.

Remove bowl from mixer and carefully fold in dry ingredients just to blend, then fold in the hot milk mixture, making sure to incorporate all the liquid. Pour batter into cake pans and bake 10 to 15 minutes until tester inserted in center comes out clean. Cool cake in pans.

Raspberry Meringue Torte continued

Meringue

Using the whip attachment whip whites, cream of tartar, and salt to soft peaks. Gradually add the sugar and whip to stiff peaks.

Assembly: Preheat oven to 500°.

Place the first layer on an oven proof plate and spread ½ of the butter cream on the first layer. Arrange 1 pint of raspberries on the butter cream and place second layer over raspberries. Repeat with second cake layer. Top with third layer and spread meringue over the entire cake. Watching closely, place in the oven and bake 2 to 3 minutes until meringue is lightly, but evenly browned. Remove from the oven and cool at room temperature for 15 minutes before serving.

Cake is best when served the day it is made.

Tangy Lemon Mousse

The Dr.s' John and Ann Havey hired our catering services throughout the year, but specifically for their annual Christmas parties. While delivering food one Christmas an employee (we know he will want to be nameless for this story) was directed to the wrong address. He carried a large tray of smoked salmon to the door, and knocked. A lady answered wearing a robe and curlers in her hair. The employee announced he was here for the party. The surprised and confused lady asked "what party?"

Meanwhile a block away, moments before the party, Dr. Havey and Nancy were pacing the drive way waiting for the smoked salmon and remaining food to arrive.

The lemon mouse, was Ann Havey's first choice for every Christmas party dessert. Even though it is a light summer dessert, garnished with fresh raspberries and mint leaves, it was a beautiful presentation on her Christmas table.

6 to 8 servings

6	egg yolks
1¾	cups granulated sugar
1½	teaspoons cornstarch
¾	cup fresh lemon juice
	Fine grated zest of 3 lemons
1	tablespoon unflavored gelatin softened in 3 tablespoons cold water
¼	cup light rum
6	egg whites
¼	cup powdered sugar
2	cups heavy cream
	Fresh strawberries or raspberries for garnish

In a non-reactive 2-quart saucepan whisk egg yolks. Gradually whisk in sugar and cornstarch until incorporated. Stir in lemon juice and zest. Bring to a boil and reduce heat to low. Cook, stirring constantly until thick and bubbly. Remove from heat and stir in the softened gelatin until dissolved, then rum. Cover and cool, stirring occasionally. Do not let custard set firm.

Tangy Lemon Mousse continued

Whip egg whites with the whip attachment on mixer to soft peaks. Slowly add the powdered sugar, whipping to a soft meringue. In another bowl whip the cream to soft peaks. Fold the whites and whipped cream into the mousse. Transfer to a serving bowl or individual dishes. Chill until firm before serving. Garnish with fresh strawberries or raspberries, and whipped cream.

The secret to a smooth creamy texture is to whip egg whites and cream to soft peaks, not stiff dry peaks.

White Chocolate Black Pepper Mousse Napoleon

We were chosen to cater desserts at an outdoor summer party for 700 guests. We created 3 choices for the hostess to choose from and this dessert was the most efficient to prepare in our time frame. In the 90° temperature we worked out of a refrigerated semi-trailer and handed trays down to the waitstaff on ground level. This is a satisfying light, cool dessert for a sultry summer night.

6 individual servings

Mousse
8	ounces quality white chocolate, preferably imported
1¼	cups heavy cream
5	tablespoons water, divided
1½	teaspoons unflavored powdered gelatin
4	egg yolks
2	tablespoons orange liqueur; Triple Sec or Grand Marnier
1	teaspoon vanilla
1	teaspoon freshly ground black pepper
1	teaspoon granulated sugar
	Fresh strawberries, blueberries, raspberries, or blackberries

Fillo Napoleons
8	fillo sheets
2	egg whites
1	tablespoon granulated sugar
4	tablespoons unsalted butter, melted
½	teaspoon vanilla

Mousse

In a bowl over hot, not boiling water, melt the white chocolate, stirring constantly to prevent burning. Set aside to cool to lukewarm.

In a mixing bowl with the wire whip attachment, whip the cream to soft peaks. Chill until ready to use.

Place 3 tablespoons of the cold water in a small, heat proof cup. Sprinkle the gelatin over the water and let stand for 3 minutes to soften. Heat 20 to 30 seconds in the microwave until all granules are dissolved. Set aside.

White Chocolate Black Pepper Mousse Napoleon continued

In another mixing bowl of a heavy-duty electric mixer, whisk together the yolks, orange liqueur, the remaining 2 tablespoons of water, black pepper and sugar. Place the bowl over a pan of hot water. The bottom of the bowl must touch the water. Whisk constantly for 3 to 5 minutes, or until the yolk mixture is light and fluffy. Mixture will be hot to the touch. Remove from heat and transfer to electric mixer. Whip with the wire whip attachment until egg mixture is tripled in volume and cool, about 5 minutes.

At low speed, stir in the dissolved gelatin just to combine. Remove from mixer. With a spatula, fold the room temperature white chocolate in to the egg mixture. Fold in the whipped cream. Cover mousse with plastic wrap and refrigerate for 2 hours until firm.

Fillo Napoleons
Preheat oven to 375°.

Whisk the whites, melted butter, and sugar to blend. Working with 4 sheets at a time, lay 4 sheets of Fillo on a flat work surface. Cover remaining sheets with plastic wrap, then cover plastic wrap with a damp cloth to prevent drying out. Brush each sheet with the butter mixture and stack together. Transfer stacked sheets to parchment-lined baking pan and brush the surface with the butter mixture. Sprinkle with granulated sugar and using a sharp knife or pizza cutter divide into 12 squares. Repeat with the remaining 4 sheets. There will be extra to allow for breakage. Bake 10 to 15 minutes until evenly browned.

Assembly: Place 1 Fillo square on a serving plate. Spoon a mound of mousse onto the square and top with another square. Repeat with mousse and top with third square. Garnish plate with assorted berries and sprinkle entire plate with powdered sugar.

Fillo should be baked on parchment or waxed paper to prevent fillo from sticking to the sheet pan. This is a more advanced recipe and should be assembled within 30 minutes of serving time. Fillo looses its crisp crunchy texture when refrigerated.

Prune Armagnac Gingerbread

I remember one summer I was making gingerbread to enter in the fair for 4-H.
Cooking and baking classes were offered to everyone and I took them all.
When I took the gingerbread out of the oven I knew I had forgotten to add the
baking soda. It was a heavy rubbery mass, so I gave it to our dog, Princess,
thinking she would eat it. Later that day I was outside and Princess came
up to me and dropped that same piece of gingerbread at my feet, turned
around and walked away coughing as she left. Of course I baked another
gingerbread, and I felt lucky when it won a blue ribbon.

The following gingerbread is completely different from what I entered
in the fair. This has a moist dense texture and a spicy flavor.
Delicious served with whipped cream.

12 servings

1	cup chopped pitted prunes
½	cup Armagnac or Cognac
1	tablespoon peeled, fine grated fresh ginger root
3	cups all-purpose flour
2	teaspoons baking soda
1	teaspoon baking powder
2	teaspoons ground cinnamon
1	teaspoon ground ginger
1	teaspoon ground cloves
⅛	teaspoon cayenne pepper
¾	teaspoon salt
1	cup unsalted butter, at room temperature
1½	cups packed light brown sugar
1	cup molasses
4	eggs
½	cup strong coffee
1	teaspoon vanilla
½	cup finely minced crystallized ginger
	Sweetened whipped cream for garnish

Preheat oven to 350°. Butter a 10-inch springform pan.

Prune Armagnac Gingerbread continued

In a saucepan cook prunes, Armagnac, and ginger root over medium heat, stirring frequently, until almost all liquid is evaporated. Remove pan from heat and let cool to room temperature.

Sift flour, soda, baking powder, cinnamon, ginger, cloves, cayenne, and salt.

In a mixing bowl with the paddle attachment, beat butter and sugar until light and fluffy. Add molasses and beat in eggs. Stir in coffee, vanilla, and crystallized ginger. Chop prunes and add to egg mixture. On low speed add sifted dry ingredients. Pour batter into prepared pan and bake 1 hour and 20 minutes, or until tester comes out clean. Cool in pan.

Gingerbread will fall slightly in center.

Susan Lipper

Mocha Prune Cake

12 servings

½   cup unsalted butter, at room temperature
1½   cups granulated sugar
3   eggs
2½   cups cake flour
1   teaspoon baking powder
1   teaspoon baking soda
1   teaspoon salt
1   teaspoon ground cinnamon
1   teaspoon ground nutmeg
1   teaspoon ground allspice
1   cup buttermilk
1   cup pitted prunes

Coffee Frosting
1   (3-ounce) package cream cheese
½   cup unsalted butter, at room temperature
1   teaspoon instant coffee granules, dissolved in 2 teaspoons hot water
1   teaspoon vanilla
1   teaspoon ground cinnamon
½   teaspoon ground allspice
2   cups powdered sugar, sifted

Cake

Preheat oven to 350°. Line 2 (9-inch) round pans with parchment paper.

Cook prunes in ½ cup water on low heat to plump. Set aside and cool to room temperature. Drain, discard liquid, and mince fine.

In a mixing bowl fitted with the paddle attachment beat the butter and sugar until light and fluffy. Beat in eggs.

Sift flour, baking powder, soda, salt, cinnamon, nutmeg, and allspice. Add buttermilk alternately with the dry ingredients, to the butter mixture, beginning and ending with the flour. Stir in the prunes. Pour into prepared pans and bake 25 to 30 minutes until a tester inserted in the center comes out clean. Cool in pans.

Mocha Prune Cake continued

Frosting
On an electric mixer using the paddle attachment beat cream cheese and butter until light and fluffy. Add dissolved coffee, vanilla, cinnamon, and allspice. On low speed stir in powdered sugar to blend, then increase speed to medium and beat until soft and fluffy. Stack cake layers together with frosting and cover cake completely with remaining frosting.

Pecan Pie Cake

16 servings

3	cups toasted pecan pieces, chopped and divided
1	cup unsalted butter, at room temperature
2	cups granulated sugar
5	egg yolks
1	tablespoon vanilla
2	cups cake flour
1	teaspoon baking soda
1	cup buttermilk
5	egg whites
¾	cup dark corn syrup

Pecan Pie Filling

½	cup firmly packed light brown sugar
¾	cup dark corn syrup
⅓	cup cornstarch
4	egg yolks
1½	cups half-and-half
¼	teaspoon salt
3	tablespoons unsalted butter
1	teaspoon vanilla

Cake

Preheat oven to 350°.

Sprinkle 2 cups pecans evenly into 3 generously buttered 9-inch round cake pans. Shake to coat bottom and sides of pans.

In a mixing bowl with the paddle attachment, beat the butter and sugar until light and fluffy. Add yolks and vanilla, continue to beat.

Sift flour and soda. Alternately add dry ingredients with buttermilk, beginning and ending with dry ingredients. Stir in remaining 1 cup pecans.

Using the wire whip attachment, whip whites to stiff peaks. Fold into the batter. Pour batter into prepared pans and bake 20 to 25 minutes, or until a tester inserted in the center comes out clean. Cool in pans. Invert onto wire cool racks and brush tops and sides with corn syrup.

Pecan Pie Cake continued

Filling

Whisk together brown sugar, corn syrup, cornstarch, yolks, half-and-half, and salt in a heavy bottomed 3-quart saucepan. Bring to a boil over medium heat, stirring constantly; boil 1 minute. Remove from heat. Whisk in butter and vanilla. Transfer to a bowl and cover surface with plastic wrap. Chill 4 hours until completely cold.

Assembly: Spread filling on each cake layer and stack together.

Cranberry Pear Ginger Upside-Down Cake

A nice fall dessert; the tart flavor of the cranberries
compliments the sweetness of the cake.

12 servings

¼	cup unsalted butter
½	cup packed light brown sugar
4	fresh pears peeled, cored, and sliced
1½	cups fresh cranberries, cleaned and chopped coarse

1½	cups cake flour
½	teaspoon ground cardamom
¼	teaspoon ground cloves
½	teaspoon ground cinnamon
¾	teaspoon baking powder
¼	teaspoon baking soda
½	teaspoon salt
½	cup unsalted butter, at room temperature
¾	cup granulated sugar
2	eggs
½	cup sour cream
1	tablespoon peeled, fine grated fresh ginger
	Sweetened whipped cream for garnish

Preheat oven to 350°.

Melt butter in a 10-inch oven proof skillet or cake pan. Add brown sugar and stir until sugar is almost dissolved. Remove from heat. Arrange sliced pears in a circular pattern with tips pointing toward the center. Sprinkle cranberries over and between the pears.

Sift flour, cardamom, cloves, cinnamon, baking powder, soda, and salt.

Using an electric mixer with the paddle attachment, beat butter and sugar until light and fluffy. Beat in eggs. Stir in sour cream and grated ginger. Mix in dry ingredients.

Spread batter over cranberries and pears. Bake 40 to 50 minutes until tester inserted in the center comes out clean. Cool in pan 5 minutes and invert onto a serving platter, scraping any glaze remaining in the pan over the cake. Serve warm or at room temperature with the sweetened whipped cream.

Buttery Shortcake

Uncle Jim relates the story about he and his father (our grandfather) picking fresh strawberries from our grandfather's patch and eating strawberries and this shortcake. His patch was reputed to be one of the best in the county.

Uncle Jim claims that during the days he courted Aunt Barbara the gift of the freshly picked strawberries won over her heart and she agreed to marry him.

8 servings

½	cup vegetable shortening
2½	cups all-purpose flour
1	tablespoon baking powder
1	teaspoon salt
⅓	cup granulated sugar
1	egg
¾	cup milk
¼	cup unsalted butter, melted

Preheat oven to 350°. Butter an 8-inch pan.

With a pastry cutter cut shortening into the flour, baking powder, salt, and sugar to a crumbly mixture. Mix the egg with the milk and add to the crumb mixture with the melted butter. Stir just to combine well. Batter will be stiff.

Spread batter evenly into prepared pan and bake 20 to 25 minutes until tester inserted in the center comes out clean and cake is light brown. Serve warm with fresh sweetened strawberries and whipped cream, or vanilla ice cream.

Shortcake is best when served with fresh hand picked strawberries at their peak of ripeness.

Aunt Betty's Orange Slice Fruitcake

In place of making the traditional fruitcake that most people generally present as gifts, Aunt Betty chose to make fruitcake without the citron,"black stuff", dried fruit peel, or molasses. This cake was anticipated by everyone during the holiday season. She packed and shipped a cake to each of her family members and friends. It is wonderful served with tea or coffee. We will always remember our special Aunt Betty when we serve this cake.

Cake

1	cup unsalted butter, at room temperature
2	cups granulated sugar
5	eggs
1	tablespoon vanilla
4	cups all-purpose flour
1	teaspoon baking soda
1	teaspoon salt
1⅓	cups buttermilk
8	ounces dates, chopped
2	cups toasted pecan pieces
1	cup flaked coconut
1	pound candied orange slices cut into 1 inch pieces
	Candied pineapple, candied cherries, and pecan halves for garnish

Orange Glaze

½	cup orange juice
½	cup granulated sugar
2	tablespoons apricot brandy, rum, or orange liqueur

Cake

Preheat oven to 350°. Butter a 10-inch tube pan.

Using an electric mixer with the paddle attachment, beat the butter and sugar until light and fluffy. Add the eggs and vanilla, continue to beat.

Sift the flour, soda, and salt. Add the dry ingredients alternately with the buttermilk, blend well. Remove from mixer and stir in the dates, pecans, coconut and candied orange pieces. Batter will be stiff.

Aunt Betty's Orange Slice Fruitcake continued

Spread in the pan evenly and decorate with candied fruits and pecans. Bake 45 to 55 minutes until cake is light brown, and tester inserted in the center comes out clean. Remove from the oven and pour glaze over the top. Run a knife around the edge and let the glaze drizzle down the sides. Cool cake in the pan. Remove from pan and wrap well. Place in the freezer for several days to age before serving.

Glaze

Stir the 3 ingredients together. Most of the sugar will dissolve when poured over the cake.

The orange slices are found in the candy aisle in the grocery store. Yes, candy companies still make these large gum drop candies.

Chocolate Mousse Torte

12 servings

Mousse

8	ounces semi-sweet chocolate, chopped
1	tablespoon instant coffee powder
¼	cup boiling water
2	tablespoons brandy
8	egg yolks
⅔	cup granulated sugar
1	teaspoon vanilla
	Dash salt
8	egg whites
½	cup heavy cream, whipped

Topping

1½	cups heavy cream
2	teaspoons vanilla
⅓	cup powdered sugar

Preheat oven to 350°. Butter a 9-inch springform pan.

Place chocolate in the top of a double boiler over hot water. Dissolve the coffee in the boiling water and pour into the chocolate. Stir until melted. Remove from heat. Set aside at room temperature.

Using the whip attachment of an electric mixer, whip the yolks and sugar until pale and tripled in volume. Remove from the mixer and fold in the vanilla and chocolate.

In another mixing bowl using a clean whip attachment, whip whites with the salt until stiff but not dry. Fold a small amount of whites into the chocolate to lighten the batter. Fold in remaining whites, folding only until no whites show. Remove 4 cups of mousse and transfer to a small bowl. Set aside. Scrape the remaining mousse into the prepared pan. Bake 25 minutes. Remove mousse from the oven and run a knife around edge to loosen. Cool to room temperature. Mousse will fall and leave a rim around the edge. Refrigerate.

To the reserved mousse, fold in the whipped cream and chill until ready to use.

Chocolate Mousse Torte continued

When the baked mousse is completely cold, place the reserved mousse in the shell of the baked mousse. Mound it slightly higher in the center, handling as little as possible. Keep refrigerated.

Topping

Using the whip attachment on an electric mixer, whip cream to stiff peaks. On low speed stir in the vanilla and sugar. Spread over the unbaked part of the mousse. For a more decorative presentation, use a pastry bag with a star tip to pipe on the whipped cream. Chill until ready to serve.

Mocha Ganache Torte

16 servings

Chocolate Ganache

2	cups heavy cream
2	ounces bittersweet or semi-sweet chocolate, chopped
1	teaspoon vanilla

Chocolate Cake

1	cup unsalted butter, at room temperature
2	cups granulated sugar
2	eggs
6	ounces bittersweet chocolate, melted
2	teaspoons vanilla
1	cup sour cream
2½	cups cake flour
2	teaspoons baking soda
½	teaspoon salt
1	cup boiling water

Coffee Butter Cream

½	cup egg whites
½	cup granulated sugar
¼	teaspoon cream of tartar
½	teaspoon salt
1	cup unsalted butter
1	tablepoon instant coffee dissolved in 2 teaspoons hot water
2	tablespoons coffee liqueur

Ganache

In a 5-quart saucepan, heat the cream to a simmer. Remove from heat. Add the chocolate and vanilla. Let set for 3 minutes and whisk until all chocolate is melted and cream is smooth. Pour into a sealed container and refrigerate overnight.

Cake

Preheat oven to 350 degrees. Line 3 (9-inch) round cake pans with parchment paper.

Mocha Ganache Torte continued

Using the paddle on an electric mixer, beat the butter and sugar until light and fluffy. Add the eggs and continue to beat. Stir in the melted chocolate, vanilla and sour cream.

Sift the flour, soda, and salt. Stir in the dry ingredients to blend, and slowly pour the boiling water into the batter, scraping down the bowl to incorporate. Batter will be thin. Pour into prepared pans and bake 20 to 25 minutes, until a tester inserted in the center comes out clean. Cool cakes in pans. At this point cakes can be wrapped and frozen until ready to use.

Butter Cream

In a mixing bowl, heat whites, sugar, cream of tartar, and salt over hot water to warm, stirring constantly. Transfer to electric mixer. Using the whip attachment, whip to stiff peaks and continue to whip until meringue has cooled to room temperature. Add butter, a piece at a time whipping until butter cream is smooth. Mixture will deflate and curdle while adding the butter, but will emulsify after all butter has been incorporated. Stir in vanilla, liquid coffee, and coffee liqueur.

Spread butter cream between cake layers. Chill while preparing ganache.

Ganache

Using the whip attachment whip chilled chocolate mixture to stiff peaks. Scrape bowl to incorporate all liquid. Cover outside of cake with ganache. Garnish cake with chocolate curls or grated chocolate if desired. Chill cake until ready to serve.

More coffee can be added to the butter cream for a stronger flavor if desired.

Ganache whips within 30 seconds to a minute. Watch closely; ganache will curdle and have a grainy texture when over whipped.

It is important to use heavy whipping cream, a light cream may not whip stiff.

Banana Crunch Cake

Many years ago our cousin, Sharon Shinn, brought iced banana bars,
that she had created, to a family reunion. She shared the recipe with us
and with a few revisions to her recipe we produced this Banana Crunch Cake.
The Pecan Nougat Crunch gives it a distinctive flavor and texture.

12 serving

Cake

2½	cups cake flour
1¼	teaspoons baking powder
1	teaspoon baking soda
½	teaspoon salt
1⅓	cups granulated sugar
1	cup unsalted butter, at room temperature
2	egg yolks
1	teaspoon vanilla
1½	cups mashed over-ripe bananas
⅔	cup buttermilk
2	egg whites

Pecan Nougat Crunch

2	cups granulated sugar
2	tablespoons water
1	cup pecan pieces

Butter Pecan Frosting

½	cup unsalted butter, at room temperature
1	(3-ounce) package cream cheese, at room temperature
2	teaspoons vanilla
4	cups powdered sugar, sifted
1	cup crushed Pecan Crunch

Cake

Preheat oven to 350°. Line 3 (9-inch) cake pans with parchment paper.

Sift flour, baking powder, soda, and salt.

Banana Crunch continued

In a mixer with the paddle attachment beat the sugar and butter until light and fluffy. Beat in the yolks and vanilla. Stir in bananas and buttermilk, then the dry ingredients.

Whip whites to soft peaks and fold into banana batter. Pour batter into prepared pans and bake 20 to 25 minutes until a tester inserted in the center comes out clean. Cool completely.

Nougat

In a heavy-bottomed saucepan heat the sugar and water over low heat until lightly caramelized and sugar is dissolved. Stir occasionally. Sugar will have some small lumps while melting. Crush with spoon and incorporate into caramel. Remove from heat and mix in the pecans. Pour out onto a parchment-lined sheet pan or a buttered sheet pan. Spread as evenly as possible and cool completely. With a mallet or rolling pin crush nougat into small pieces.

Frosting

Using the paddle attachment on an electric mixer, beat butter and cream cheese until fluffy. On low speed add vanilla and powdered sugar. If needed, add milk to desired spreading consistency. Frost cake and sprinkle Pecan Crunch over entire cake.

Key Lime Cheesecake

16 servings

Crust

1½	cups graham cracker crumbs
¼	cup packed brown sugar
6	tablespoons unsalted butter, melted

Filling

3	pounds (6 8-ounce packages) cream cheese
1¾	cups granulated sugar
5	eggs
¼	cup heavy cream
¾	cup bottled key lime juice
	Fine grated zest of 1 lime

Crust

Preheat oven to 350°.

Mix crust ingredients and press into a 10-inch springform pan. Set aside.

Filling

Using the paddle attachment on an electric mixer, beat cream cheese and sugar until smooth and fluffy, scraping down bowl 2 times. Beat in eggs, scrape down bowl. Stir in cream, lime juice and zest. Pour into crust and bake 40 to 45 minutes. Cake will raise, be soft and wobbly, but feel firm to the touch. Turn oven off and let rest in oven for 10 minutes.

Remove from oven and run a thin bladed knife around edge to loosen, to hinder cracking in the center. Cool to room temperature, cover with plastic wrap and chill over night before serving.

Place a pan of hot water in the oven while baking cheesecake. This prevents cake from drying out.

Blackberry Pinwheel Cobbler

One summer at farmers market in Columbia, Missouri a lovely couple that had fresh wild blackberries for sale shared this recipe from a farmers magazine. The cobbler is delicious served with cream, crème fraîche, or ice cream.

12 servings

1½	cups granulated sugar
2	cups water
1	cup unsalted butter, divided
1½	cups self-rising flour
⅓	cup milk
5	cups fresh or frozen blackberries
1	teaspoon ground cinnamon

Preheat oven to 350°.

Combine sugar and water in a 2 quart saucepan; stir well. Boil over medium heat until sugar dissolves. Set aside at room temperature.

Place ½ cup butter in a 9x13-inch baking pan in the oven for 3 minutes until melted. Set aside.

Cut remaining ½ cup butter into flour until mixture resembles coarse crumbs. Add milk, stirring just until dry ingredients are moistened. Turn dough out onto a lightly floured surface, and knead lightly 4 or 5 times just to form a dough.

Roll dough into a 12x9 inch rectangle. Arrange 3 cups of blackberries over dough and sprinkle with cinnamon. Scatter remaining berries in the 9x13-inch pan of butter. Roll dough up jellyroll fashion. Cut roll into 12 pieces, placing cut side down, over berries. Pour sugar syrup around pieces and bake 50 to 55 minutes, until golden and bubbly. Serve warm.

Black Bottom Coconut Cream Pie

8 to 10 servings

Crust

1½	cups graham cracker crumbs
¼	cup granulated sugar
½	cup unsalted butter, melted
½	cup finely chopped toasted almonds
½	cup flaked coconut

Ganache

⅓	cup heavy whipping cream
2	ounces bittersweet or semi-sweet chocolate, chopped
1	teaspoon vanilla

Coconut Filling

2	cups milk
2	tablespoons granulated sugar
1	can (14-ounces) cream of coconut
3	eggs
3	egg yolks
⅓	cup cornstarch
¼	teaspoon salt
3	tablespoons unsalted butter
1	tablespoon vanilla
½	teaspoon coconut extract
½	cup flaked coconut

Garnish

1½	cups heavy cream
¼	cup powdered sugar
2	teaspoons vanilla
½	cup flaked coconut, lightly toasted
	Toasted sliced almonds

Black Bottom Coconut Cream Pie continued

Crust

Preheat oven to 350°.

Combine the graham cracker crumbs with the remaining ingredients and press into a 9-inch pie pan. Bake 6 to 8 minutes or until edges are browned. Cool completely.

Ganache

In a 2-quart saucepan bring cream to a boil. Add the chocolate and vanilla and whisk until melted and smooth. Cool slightly before pouring into the cooled pie shell. Refrigerate until firm.

Filling

In a 2-quart saucepan combine the milk and sugar, heat over medium heat until sugar is dissolved. Continue to cook until the mixture comes to a boil.

While the milk is heating, whisk together the cream of coconut, eggs, egg yolks, cornstarch and salt. Slowly pour half of the hot milk mixture into the eggs whisking constantly. Return the egg mixture to the pan, whisking to combine. Cook over medium heat, stirring constantly, until custard boils.

Remove from heat and whisk in the butter, vanilla, coconut extract, and coconut. Transfer custard to a bowl and cover surface with plastic wrap. Refrigerate until firm and cold.

Spread coconut filling over the chocolate ganache. Chill.

Garnish

Using the wire whip attachment on an electric mixer whip the cream to stiff peaks. Whisk in the sugar and vanilla. Using a decorating tube with a star tip, pipe the cream over the filling, or spread cream over filling. Sprinkle with the almonds and coconut. Chill until ready to serve.

Raspberry Walnut Tart

Peggy Glenn, from Boone County National Bank was one of our faithful customers in Columbia, Missouri. She ordered the tart on many different occasions, and declared this one of her favorite desserts. She informed us that with the addition of whipped cream and caramel rum sauce the dessert was even better. During our first catering experience at furniture market we presented the tart as a dessert selection. After having it for dessert HC Haynes, a representative for Kessler Industries, came back into the kitchen, threw up his hands exclaiming it was a religious experience. We still laugh about that moment.

8 servings

Crust

1	cup all-purpose flour
⅓	cup powdered sugar
½	cup unsalted butter, at room temperature
¼	teaspoon salt

Filling

20	ounces Individually Quick Frozen raspberries, without sugar
¾	cup coarse chopped English Walnuts
2	eggs
1	cup granulated sugar
1	teaspoon vanilla
½	teaspoon salt
½	teaspoon baking powder
¼	cup all-purpose flour

Preheat oven to 350°.

With a pastry blender cut flour, sugar, and butter to a crumb mixture. Gather into a ball and press into a 10-inch tart pan or a 9x13-inch pan. Bake 15 minutes until light golden. Cool.

Arrange frozen raspberries and walnuts over cooled crust.

Using a whip attachment on an electric mixer, whip eggs, sugar, and vanilla until light and fluffy. Remove from the mixer and stir in the salt, baking powder, and flour with a spatula. Pour over the raspberries and walnuts to cover. Bake 30 to 35 minutes until golden brown.

Serve warm drizzled with caramel sauce and a mound of whipped cream.

COOKIES, CANDIES, AND SWEET TREATS

Ginger Snaps with Pumpkin Dip

These crisp, but chewy ginger cookies are a wonderful autumn snack
served with the pumpkin dip and hot spiced apple cider.

4 dozen cookies

Cookies

1½	cups vegetable shortening
2	cups granulated sugar
2	eggs
½	cup molasses
1	teaspoon vanilla
4	cups unbleached all-purpose flour
2	tablespoons ground ginger
1	tablespoon baking soda
2	teaspoons ground cinnamon
1	teaspoon salt

In a mixing bowl using the paddle attachment, beat the shortening and sugar until
fluffy. Add eggs and beat well. Stir in the molasses and vanilla. Blend in the flour,
ginger, soda, cinnamon, and salt. Chill dough 30 minutes.

Preheat oven to 350°.

Roll dough into 1-inch balls and roll in granulated sugar. Place cookies on a
parchment lined baking sheet and flatten slightly. Bake 12 to 15 minutes until
cookies are brown around edges and domed in center.

Pumpkin Dip

about 5 cups

4	cups powdered sugar, sifted
1	pound cream cheese, at room temperature
1	(16-ounce) can pumpkin purée
2	teaspoons ground cinnamon
1	teaspoon ground ginger

In a mixing bowl beat the sugar and cream cheese until fluffy. Stir in the pumpkin,
cinnamon, and ginger until mixture is smooth. Chill until ready to serve.

White Chocolate Chip Coconut Pecan Cookies

24 cookies

1	cup unsalted butter, at room temperature
⅔	cup granulated sugar
⅔	cup packed light brown sugar
2	eggs
2	teaspoons vanilla
2	cups unbleached all-purpose flour
1	teaspoon baking soda
½	teaspoon salt
2	cups toasted flake coconut
1½	cups white chocolate chips
1	cup toasted pecan pieces

Preheat oven to 350°.

Lightly toast coconut and pecans about 5 to 10 minutes until coconut becomes light golden in color. Set aside to cool to room temperature.

In a mixing bowl with the paddle attachment, beat the butter and sugars until light and fluffy. Beat in the eggs and vanilla. Stir in flour, soda, salt, and coconut to blend. Remove from the mixer and add the white chocolate chips and pecans. Drop by teaspoons onto a parchment-lined sheet pan and bake 8 to 10 minutes until cookies have puffed and are golden brown.

Butter Cut Out Cookies

Enclosed in a valentine card I received from a friend in sixth grade, was this recipe and a small plastic red heart shaped cookie cutter. The recipe yielded 6 cookies. We have made several thousand of these cookies since sixth grade. They are a tender and buttery.

24 cookies

¾	cup unsalted butter, at room temperature
¾	cup powdered sugar, sifted
2	egg yolks
2	teaspoons vanilla
2	cups unbleached all-purpose flour
¼	teaspoon salt

Glaze
2	cups powdered sugar
2-4	tablespoons water
½	teaspoon vanilla

Cookies

In a mixing bowl with the paddle attachment, beat the butter and powdered sugar until fluffy. Add the yolks and vanilla, and stir in the flour and salt to form dough. Wrap in plastic wrap and chill 30 minutes.

Preheat oven to 350°. Roll dough out on a floured surface to ¼ in thick. Cut into desired shapes and place on a parchment-lined baking sheet. Bake 10 to 12 minutes just until the edges are brown. Cool.

Glaze

Prepare the glaze by mixing the powdered sugar with the water and vanilla to a desired consistency for dipping cookies. Dip cookies and place on a cooling rack to dry.

Nancy (Lipper) Pierron

Candied Fruit Slices

This is a wonderful holiday butter cookie.

48 cookies

1	cup unsalted butter, at room temperature
1	cup powdered sugar
1	egg
1	teaspoon vanilla
2¼	cups unbleached all-purpose flour
1	cup toasted pecan halves
2	cups candied red and green cherries

Beat butter and powdered sugar until pale and fluffy. Add egg and vanilla, continue to beat. Stir in the flour to blend well, then add pecans and cherries. Chill dough 1 hour.

Divide dough in thirds and shape into logs 12-inches long. Wrap in plastic wrap; chill at least 2 or 3 hours.

Preheat oven to 325°.

Slice logs into ¼-inch slices and place on parchment paper lined baking pan. Bake 13 to 15 minutes until lightly browned around edges and firm in the center.

These are nice to have available in the freezer to slice and bake for a holiday cookie exchange, or for a spur-of-the-moment cookie tray.

Fruitcake Cookies

Easier to bake than fruitcakes, and almost as flavorful. Bake cookies in October or November to let the flavors mellow before the holidays.

12 dozen

6	cups toasted pecan pieces
2	pounds candied red and green cherries, halved
8	ounces golden raisins
8	ounces dates, chopped
½	cup all-purpose flour
3½	cups all-purpose flour
1½	teaspoons baking soda
1½	teaspoons ground cinnamon
1½	teaspoons ground allspice
1½	teaspoons ground cloves
1½	teaspoons ground nutmeg
1	teaspoon salt
1	cup unsalted butter, at room temperature
2¼	cups packed light brown sugar
6	eggs
1½	cups whiskey

Preheat oven to 350°.

In a large bowl mix to coat the pecans, cherries, raisins, and dates with the ½ cup flour, separating any fruit than has clumped together. Set aside.

Sift the 3½ cups flour, soda, cinnamon, allspice, cloves, nutmeg, and salt in another bowl.

In a mixing bowl with the paddle attachment, beat the butter and brown sugar until light and fluffy. Add the eggs one at a time, beating well after each addition. Stir in the dry ingredients alternately with the whiskey. Blend in the fruit mixture and stir to completely coat fruit.

Drop by a teaspoon onto a parchment-lined baking sheet one-inch apart. Bake 8 to 10 minutes until cookies are firm in the center and golden brown around the edges. Cool and layer cookies between sheets of parchment paper in an airtight container. Store in a cool dry place for several months.

Hazelnut Chocolate Sable Cookies

Pronounced (sab-lay) these cookies are crisp and crunchy, nice to serve with tea.

3 dozen cookies

1	cup toasted hazelnuts, ground fine
6	ounces bittersweet chocolate
1¾	cups powdered sugar
10	ounces (1 cup plus 2 tablespoons) unsalted butter at room temperature
1	tablespoon fine grated orange zest
2	eggs
1	tablespoon vanilla
½	teaspoon salt
3	cups all-purpose flour

Chop or grate chocolate by hand to the size of rice grains and mix with the ground hazelnuts.

Beat powdered sugar, butter, orange zest, eggs, and vanilla until smooth. Stir in chocolate and nut mixture with flour and salt. Chill until firm.

Preheat oven to 350°. Roll dough out to the thickness of ¼-inch and cut into circles or desired shapes.

These cookies are delectable as they are, but a more elegant presentation is to sandwich them with melted chocolate.

Shortbread

On my first visit to Greensboro, Nancy took me to the Old Mill of Guilford. While chatting with co-owner Heidi Parnell, she gave me helpful suggestions on making shortbread. Her secret to the perfect shortbread is using equal amounts of rice flour and all-purpose flour, resulting in a sandy, but tender texture. I have used the following shortbread for many years and adapted it to be as close to the firm, crisp, but tender shortbread that my friend Dorell Kirschner brought back from Scotland several years ago.

36 cookies

1⅓	cups unsalted butter, at room temperature
⅔	cup sugar
¾	teaspoon vanilla
½	teaspoon salt
1⅓	cups rice flour
2	cups unbleached all-purpose flour

Preheat oven to 350°.

Cream butter, sugar, and vanilla until smooth, but not fluffy. Stir in salt, all-purpose flour and rice flour to incorporate. Dough will be dry and crumbly. Add a tablespoon of butter if dough does not form. Form dough into a disk and chill 20 minutes to firm.

Roll dough to the thickness of ¼-inch, cut into desired shapes and place on a parchment lined pan. Bake 12 to 15 minutes until firm in the center and the edges are just starting to brown.

Shortbread can also be dipped in milk or semi-sweet chocolate and sprinkled with toasted chopped nuts.

Old Mill of Guilford
1340 N. C. 68 North Oak Ridge, N. C. 27310
Phone 910-643-4783

Susan Lipper

Mexican Shortbread Cookies

Cookies are delicate, tender, and delicious.

24 cookies

½   cup almonds
1¾ cups all-purpose flour (weight 8-ounces)
7½ teaspoons granulated sugar
¼   teaspoon salt
1   teaspoon baking powder
2   tablespoons unsalted butter, at room temperature
2   tablespoons vegetable shortening

Toast almonds about 10 minutes until golden. Place the flour in a baking dish and toast to a deep creamy color 10 to 15 minutes. Cool completely. Grind the almonds with the sugar to a fine powder, but not a paste.

Make a well in the center of the flour, salt, and baking powder. Add the ground nut mixture, butter, and shortening and blend until mixture is crumbly, like a pie crust. Press crumbs lightly together and wrap in plastic wrap. Chill 2 hours.

Preheat oven to 350°.

Roll dough between 2 pieces of parchment paper to ¼-thick. The dough will be crumbly around the edges. Cut cookies in desired shapes and place on parchment paper. Press dough together, cut more cookies. Handle dough as little as possible to prevent tough cookies when baked.

Bake at 350° 10 to 15 minutes until pale golden around edges. Sprinkle with powder sugar while hot. Cool and store in an airtight container.

Danish Butter Cookies

24 to 36 cookies depending on the size

Cookies

1	cup unsalted butter, at room temperature
¾	cup packed light brown sugar
1	egg yolk
1	teaspoon vanilla
2¼	cups unbleached all-purpose flour

Browned Butter Icing

3	tablespoons unsalted butter
1	teaspoon vanilla
1-2	tablespoons milk
1½	cups powdered sugar

Cookies

Beat the butter and sugar until fluffy. Add yolk and vanilla and stir in flour to blend. Chill dough until slightly firm. Divide dough in half and roll into logs. The thicker the log the larger the cookie. Wrap well in plastic wrap and chill or freeze logs.

Preheat oven to 300°. Line a baking sheet with parchment paper.

Cut logs into ⅛-inch thin slice. Slightly press the cookies with an indentation, using a fork blade, for a decorative design. Bake cookies 8-10 minutes until firm. Do not brown. Cool.

Icing

In a heavy-bottomed saucepan, over medium heat, cook the butter to a light golden brown. Remove from heat and add vanilla and milk. Beat in powdered sugar until smooth. Add more milk, if needed for easier spreading consistency. Sandwich cookies with icing.

Dutch Almond Pastry

Cora Van Wyke from Pella, Iowa gave me this recipe when we were in college together. Another friend, Gloria, and her family have often asked me to make "those almond things" because they are a favorite treat at Christmas time. This recipe is more commonly known as Dutch Letters.

About 24 pastries, depending on the size

Pastry

1	pound cold unsalted butter
2	cups all-purpose flour
2	cups cake flour
½	teaspoon salt
1	cup cold water

Filling

3	large eggs
3	cups granulated sugar
1	teaspoon almond extract
2	(8-ounces cans) almond paste

Pastry

Use a pastry blender to cut butter into flour and salt until crumbly and butter is the size of peas. Add water, and mix thoroughly until dough forms a ball. Chill at least 8 hours or overnight.

In a separate bowl, beat eggs and sugar together, then add almond extract and almond paste. Mix together thoroughly and chill at least 8 hours or overnight.

Preheat oven to 350°. Line 2 baking sheets with parchment paper.

Divide dough into 8 pieces. Work on one piece at a time, and leave remaining sections in the refrigerator. On a lightly floured surface, roll each piece into a rectangle shape, folding and rolling 2 times; this creates flakiness during baking. Form a log of paste filling (about the size of a hot dog) along one long edge of pastry, and roll jellyroll fashion into a long log. Shape into letters, such as C, L, S,

Dutch Almond Pastry continued

or O for ease in handling. Brush with a small amount of water to seal and press edges firmly. Use a fork to make holes in the top of log to allow steam to escape while baking. Chill while rolling out remaining sections of dough. Bake about 20 to 25 minutes or until golden brown.

Refrigerating pastry after shaping helps prevent filling from spilling out while baking. A regular sized baking sheet will hold 3 or 4 pieces of pastry.

Patricia (Lipper) Self

Orange Almond Biscotti

48 biscotti

2	eggs
1	egg yolk
1	teaspoon vanilla
1	tablespoon fine grated orange zest
1	cup granulated sugar
2	cups unbleached all-purpose flour
1	teaspoon baking soda
¼	teaspoon salt
1½	cups natural whole almonds, toasted and coarsely chopped

Preheat oven to 300°.

In the bowl of an electric mixer fitted with the paddle attachment stir the eggs, yolk, vanilla, orange zest and sugar. Add the flour, soda, salt, and almonds, stirring until dough is formed.

Turn the dough out onto a lightly floured surface, knead it several times, and divide it in half. Roll each piece into a 12-inch log. Arrange the logs at least 3-inches apart on a parchment-lined baking sheet and flatten slightly. Bake 30 minutes. Remove from the oven and cool on the pan for 10 minutes.

On a cutting board cut the logs crosswise ½-inch thick, and return to the baking sheet placing cut side down. Bake in the 300° oven for 15 minutes. Let cool and store in an airtight container.

Spicy Nut Biscotti

This biscotti is our personal favorite because they are not as
hard as other biscotti, but tender and crisp.

32 biscotti

½	cup unsalted butter, at room temperature
1	cup granulated sugar
2	eggs
2	teaspoons fine grated orange zest
1	teaspoon fine grated lemon zest
1½	teaspoons vanilla
2	cups unbleached all-purpose flour
½	teaspoon baking soda
½	teaspoon baking powder
¼	teaspoon salt
2	teaspoons freshly ground black pepper
½	cup toasted pine nuts
1	cup toasted walnuts, coarsely chopped.

Preheat oven to 350°.

In a mixing bowl fitted with the paddle attachment, beat butter and sugar until
light and fluffy. Add the eggs, orange and lemon zests, and vanilla. Stir in the
flour, soda, baking powder, salt, and pepper. Mix in the pine nuts and walnuts,
stirring just to blend.

Divide dough in half and form into 2 (12-inch) logs. Arrange on a parchment-lined
baking sheet and flatten slightly. Bake logs 20 to 25 minutes, or until they are pale
golden and firm in the center. Cool on the baking sheet for 10 minutes.

On a cutting board cut the logs ½-inch thick and return to the baking sheet placing
the cut sides down. Bake 8 minutes on each side, or until they are pale golden.
Let biscotti cool to room temperature and store in an airtight container.

Biscotti retain flavor 2 to 3 weeks stored in an airtight container.

Cream Cheese Brownies

12 brownies

Filling

8	ounces cream cheese, at room temperature
¼	cup unsalted butter, at room temperature
¼	cup granulated sugar
2	eggs
1	teaspoon vanilla
1	tablespoon all-purpose flour

Brownie

1	cup unsalted butter
6	ounces semi-sweet chocolate, chopped
4	eggs
1¾	cups granulated sugar
2	teaspoons vanilla
¾	teaspoon salt
1½	cups all-purpose flour
3	tablespoons cocoa
1½	cups toasted pecan pieces

Cream Cheese Filling

Beat cream cheese, butter, and sugar until smooth. Add eggs and vanilla to blend, stir in the flour and set aside.

Brownies

Preheat oven to 350°. Butter a 9x13-inch pan.

Melt butter and chocolate in a bowl over a pan of hot water stirring until smooth. Set aside. Stir eggs, sugar, and vanilla together; mix in chocolate mixture. Sift together flour, salt, and cocoa. Stir into chocolate mixture with nuts. Spread ½ of the chocolate batter in the prepared pan. Spread the cheese filling over the batter and cover with remaining chocolate batter. Bake 25 to 30 minutes until a tester inserted in the center comes out clean. Cool and cut into 12 squares.

Chocolate Macaroon Brownies

Use the Cream Cheese Brownie batter and layer with coconut macaroon filling.

12 Brownies

2	egg whites
½	cup granulated sugar
1	teaspoon vanilla
½	teaspoon coconut extract
2	cups flake coconut
1	tablespoon all-purpose flour

Preheat oven to 350°. Butter a 9x13-inch baking pan.

Using the wire whip attachment on the mixer, whip whites and vanilla to soft peaks. Add sugar gradually and whip until stiff. Remove from mixer and fold in coconut and flour. Spread enough chocolate batter to cover the bottom of the prepared pan. Distribute the coconut mixture over the batter, then spread remaining brownie batter over coconut mixture. Bake 25 to 30 minutes until a tester inserted in the center comes out clean.

Coconut Macaroon Bars

24 bars

2¾	cups graham cracker crumbs
½	cup finely chopped almonds
⅓	cup powdered sugar
6	tablespoons unsalted butter, melted
1	(14-ounce) bag flake coconut
1	(14-ounce) can sweetened condensed milk
1	teaspoon coconut extract
6	ounces semi-sweet chocolate
2	teaspoons unsalted butter
	Additional toasted chopped almonds for garnish

Preheat oven to 350°. Butter a 9x13-inch pan

In a mixing bowl combine cracker crumbs and sugar. Add the butter and stir to combine. Press crust mixture firmly on bottom of the prepared pan. Set aside.

Sprinkle coconut evenly over crust. Stir condensed milk and coconut extract together and pour evenly over the crust to completely cover coconut. Bake 25 minutes until set but not brown. Cool completely.

In a saucepan, over low heat, melt chocolate with the 2 teaspoons butter. Spread or drizzle evenly over the bars, sprinkle with additional almonds and chill until firm. Cut into 24 bars. Store in an airtight container in the refrigerator.

Snickerdoodles

I have made this recipe for over 20 years, and it is still a favorite. I took these to a bake sale fund-raiser where I work, and a man bought a dozen cookies at one time. He said Snickerdoodles were his favorite, but his wife had lost her recipe.

5 dozen

1	cup soft vegetable shortening
1½	cups granulated sugar
2	eggs
2¾	cups sifted all-purpose flour
2	teaspoons cream of tartar
1	teaspoon baking soda
½	teaspoon salt

Cinnamon Sugar

2	tablespoons sugar
2	tablespoons cinnamon

Cream butter and sugar together until smooth; add eggs and mix thoroughly. Sift together and stir in dry ingredients. Mix thoroughly until dough forms a ball. Chill dough for 8 hours or overnight.

Preheat oven to 400°.

Roll into balls the size of small walnuts. Roll balls in cinnamon-sugar mixture and place about 2-inches apart on a parchment-lined baking sheet. Bake 8 to 10 minutes until lightly brown, but still soft.

I like to use stoneware-baking sheets instead of metal. I have found that the cookies need to bake a little longer, about 2 to 3 minutes more. The outside will be crisp, but the center will still be slightly soft.

Patricia (Lipper) Self

Chocolate Peanut Butter Swirl Fudge

This is from our Aunt Betty Harris. She made this at Christmas for special gift packages. This is an alternative for those who love peanut butter cups.

3	cups granulated sugar
1	tablespoon light corn syrup
4	tablespoons cocoa powder
7	marshmallows or a hand-full of miniature marshmallows
1	cup milk
2	teaspoons vanilla extract
1	cup peanut butter, or as much as desired

In a 4-quart heavy bottom saucepan mix all ingredients, except peanut butter. Stirring constantly brings to a boil over medium heat. Reduce heat to low and cook to soft ball stage, 232° on a candy thermometer.

Remove from heat and plunge pan in a bowl of cold water to stop cooking process. Cool about 5 minutes then beat fudge until creamy. Pour out onto a buttered surface and knead with buttered hands. Pat fudge into 2 rectangles on 2 parchment-lined pans and spread each one with ½ of the peanut butter. Roll into a pinwheel and chill before slicing into thin individual pieces.

Pralines

2½ pounds

1	cup packed light brown sugar
2	cups granulated sugar
3	tablespoons light corn syrup
¼	teaspoon salt
1	cup heavy cream
4	tablespoons unsalted butter
2	teaspoons vanilla extract
1½	cups toasted pecan halves

Combine the sugars, corn syrup, salt, and cream in a heavy 5-quart saucepan. Cook over medium heat, stirring constantly to dissolve sugar. Stop stirring once candy has boiled. Cook to soft ball stage, 232° on a candy thermometer. Remove from heat and let stand undisturbed for five minutes to cool. Add vanilla and beat until creamy. Stir in pecans and quickly drop by teaspoons onto parchment paper.

If candy begins to harden add a teaspoon of cream and reheat to soften. Before pralines set press a pecan half in the center of each candy. Store in a sealed container.

This recipe can be doubled, but be sure a friend is available to help. One person cannot dip candies fast enough before candy hardens.

Minted Walnuts

These are a different version from the usual mint candies at receptions.
They are also a nice addition to Christmas gift packages.

1½ pounds

¼   cup Karo white corn syrup
1   cup granulated sugar
½   cup water
1   teaspoon peppermint extract
10   marshmallows
3   cups (10-ounce package) English walnut halves

Combine syrup, sugar, and water in a 4-quart saucepan. Stirring constantly, bring to a boil. Cook undisturbed to soft ball stage; 238° on a candy thermometer. Remove from heat, add marshmallows and peppermint extract. Stir until melted. Add walnuts and stir to coat nuts. Pour onto waxed paper or a buttered pan and spread out as much as possible. Let candy cool and dry before separating into individual pieces.

Store in a sealed container at room temperature.

By adding a drop of any food coloring you can change the color for any season or occasion. Candy should harden within a day depending on the humidity level. Try to avoid making candy on humid days, as drying time will extend to two days.

Buttermilk Fudge

This is Hazel Jean Davis' favorite recipe that we have made almost every Christmas for the past 30 years. It is rich, creamy, and delicious. Worth the effort!

2 pounds

1	cup buttermilk
2	cups granulated sugar
2	tablespoons Karo white corn syrup
½	cup unsalted butter
1	teaspoon baking soda
¼	teaspoon salt
2	teaspoons vanilla
2	cups toasted pecan pieces
	Additional toasted pecan halves

Mix buttermilk, sugar, syrup, butter, and salt in a 5-quart heavy-bottomed saucepan. Stirring constantly over medium heat bring to a boil. Add the baking soda and continue to cook stirring constantly. Cook to soft ball stage, 232°, on a candy thermometer. Remove pan from heat and plunge into a bowl of cold water to stop cooking process. Cool 5 minutes. Remove pan from water, add the vanilla and beat. The candy is a sticky gooey glob. Scrap hardened candy from pan while beating. When candy begins to loose its gloss quickly beat in pecans.

With a teaspoon, working quickly, spoon small mounds onto parchment paper. Place a pecan half on each candy while still soft. Let fudge harden at room temperature. Store candies in a sealed airtight container.

Beating time for this fudge is long and strenuous. With the help of another person to beat the fudge, your arm will not feel quite so strained.

Snickers Bars

We had made these bars once and then forgot about them until
a friend of ours, Joan Johnson, requested them. She remembered how
she had enjoyed them and asked for the recipe. After diligently
searching we found an old torn copy hidden away.

24 to 36 pieces depending on size

Bottom Layer

1	cup milk chocolate chips
¼	cup peanut butter
¼	cup butterscotch chips

Second Layer

1	cup granulated sugar
¼	cup butter
¼	cup milk
¼	cup peanut butter
1	cup marshmallow crème
1	teaspoon vanilla
1	cup roasted peanuts

Third Layer

20	caramels
2	tablespoon hot water

Fourth Layer

1	cup milk chocolate chips
1	cup peanut butter
¼	cup butterscotch chips

Bottom Layer

Line a 9x13-inch pan with parchment paper.

In a bowl heat all 3 ingredients over a pan of hot water. Stir until completely
smooth. Spread in the prepared pan and chill until firm.

Snickers Bars continued

Second Layer

Bring sugar, butter, and milk to a boil. Cook 5 minutes. Over low heat add the peanut butter, marshmallow crème, and vanilla. Pour over the first layer and sprinkle with the peanuts. Chill.

Third Layer

In a bowl over hot water or in the microwave melt the caramels and water. Drizzle over the Second Layer. Chill.

Fourth Layer

In a bowl over hot water stir all 3 ingredients until melted. Cool slightly before spreading on top. Chill until bars are completely firm.

Unmold by running a knife around the edges. Flip out onto a parchment-lined sheet and invert again onto another lined sheet so candy is upright. Cut into individual pieces and store in an airtight container in the refrigerator.

Butter Toffee

We acquired this recipe in the mid 1960's. Our family was invited to Bud and Lola Eder's home to watch the New Years Day Parade; they had the only color TV in the neighborhood. This toffee was part of the holiday treats Lola prepared. Many toffee recipes can be found, but this is the one we have always made.

2 pounds

2¼	cups granulated sugar
½	cup water
1	teaspoon salt
1	cup unsalted butter
1	cup coarsely chopped or slivered toasted almonds
1	cup semi-sweet chocolate chips
	Additional chopped toasted almonds

Combine sugar, salt, water, and butter in a 4-quart heavy-bottomed saucepan, and bring to a boil, stirring constantly over medium heat. Cook to 260° and add chopped almonds. Continue to cook to hard crack stage, 300°, stirring constantly. Reduce heat if toffee starts to smoke and darken to quickly.

Pour onto a parchment lined cookie sheet spreading as thin as desired. Sprinkle with the chocolate chips and let set to melt. Spread over toffee to coat and sprinkle with additional chopped almonds. Set aside to harden, and break into small pieces. Store in an airtight container.

Avoid making toffee on a humid day. Cooking time is longer and the toffee has a bitter flavor.

EQUIVALENCIES AND SUBSTITUTIONS

A dash (or pinch)	equals less than ⅛ teaspoon
3 teaspoons	equal 1 tablespoon
2 tablespoons	equal ⅛ cup
4 tablespoons	equal ¼ cup
5⅓ tablespoons	equal ⅓ cup
8 tablespoons	equal ½ cup
10⅔ tablespoons	equal ⅔ cup
12 tablespoons	equal ¾ cup
16 tablespoons	equal 1 cup

1 pound of granulated sugar	equals 2 cups
1 pound of brown sugar	equals 2¼ cups packed brown sugar
1 cup of granulated sugar	equals 1⅓ cups packed brown sugar
1 pound of powdered sugar	equals 2¼ cups
1 pound of all-purpose flour	equals 4 cups
12 to 14 egg yolks	equal 1 cup
8 to 10 egg whites	equal 1 cup
12-13 egg whites	equal 1½ cups
1 clove of garlic	equals ⅛ teaspoon garlic powder
1 lemon	equals 2½ to 3 tablespoon juice
1 package-unflavored gelatin	equals 2 teaspoons

When you are out of....	Substitute.....
1 tablespoon of baking powder	1 teaspoon of baking soda and 2 teaspoons of cream of tartar
1 tablespoon of cornstarch (for thickening)	2 tablespoons of flour
1 cup milk	½ cup of evaporated milk and ½ cup of water
1 cup of buttermilk (or sour milk)	1 cup of milk mixed with 1 tablespoon of vinegar or lemon juice (let stand 5 minutes)
sour cream	use yogurt for a healthier lower fat ingredient
1 cup of sugar	1 cup of honey (reduce other liquid in recipe by ¼ cup)
Self-rising flour (1 cup)	1 cup all-purpose flour, 1 teaspoon baking powder, and ½ teaspoon salt
Ginger ale	mix equal parts of Coca-Cola with 7-up

HANDY HINTS

Fresh eggs float in salted water, but old eggs sink-they should be discarded.

1 teaspoon of lemon juice added to rice while cooking results in fluffier whiter rice.

Keep in mind 8 ounces uncooked spaghetti makes 4 cups cooked.

Marinate red meats in wine to tenderize.

To keep potatoes from budding place an apple in the bag with them.

Dust nuts in flour to keep them from settling to the bottom of batters while baking.

A splash of balsamic vinegar or fresh lemon juice enhances the flavor of fresh strawberries.

Cookie dough can be frozen up to 3 months in an airtight container or refrigerated 3 to 4 days.

For an instant white sauce blend together 1 cup soft butter and 1 cup all-purpose flour. Spread in an ice cube tray and freeze. Store cubes in a plastic bag in the freezer. For a medium-thick sauce drop 1 cube into 1 cup of milk and heat slowly, stirring as it thickens.

Store carton of cottage cheese upside down. It will keep twice as long.

1 pound of butter will yield 50 pats.

1 quart of whipping cream will yield dollops for 50 guests.

1 pound of coffee will yield 50 cups.

3 gallons of punch will serve 50 guests.

4 gallons of iced tea will serve 50 guests.

1 lemon will yield 8 slices for 8 glasses of iced tea.

INDEX

INDEX

INDEX

ORDER FORMS

Le Petit Market
213 South Elm St.
Greensboro, N.C. 27401
Phone (336)274-8646
Email: lepetitmarket@yahoo.com

Please send_____copy(ies) of *The Sister's Secrets: A Collection of Timeless Recipes.*

Per copy	$24.95	_____
Postage per copy	$ 3.95	_____
Sales tax	6%	_____
	Total	_____

Check method of payment:

☐ Visa   ☐ Mastercard   ☐ Check   ☐ Money Order

Cardholder's signature_____ Expiration _____

Mail cookbook to:

Name _____

Address _____

City _____ State_____ Zip Code_____

Your Phone number _____

Le Petit Market
213 South Elm St.
Greensboro, N.C. 27401
Phone (336)274-8646
Email: lepetitmarket@yahoo.com

Please send_____copy(ies) of *The Sister's Secrets: A Collection of Timeless Recipes.*

Per copy	$24.95	_____
Postage per copy	$ 3.95	_____
Sales tax	6%	_____
	Total	_____

Check method of payment:

☐ Visa   ☐ Mastercard   ☐ Check   ☐ Money Order

Cardholder's signature_____ Expiration _____

Mail cookbook to:

Name _____

Address _____

City _____ State_____ Zip Code_____

Your Phone number _____